Eyewitness
ANCIENT EGYPT

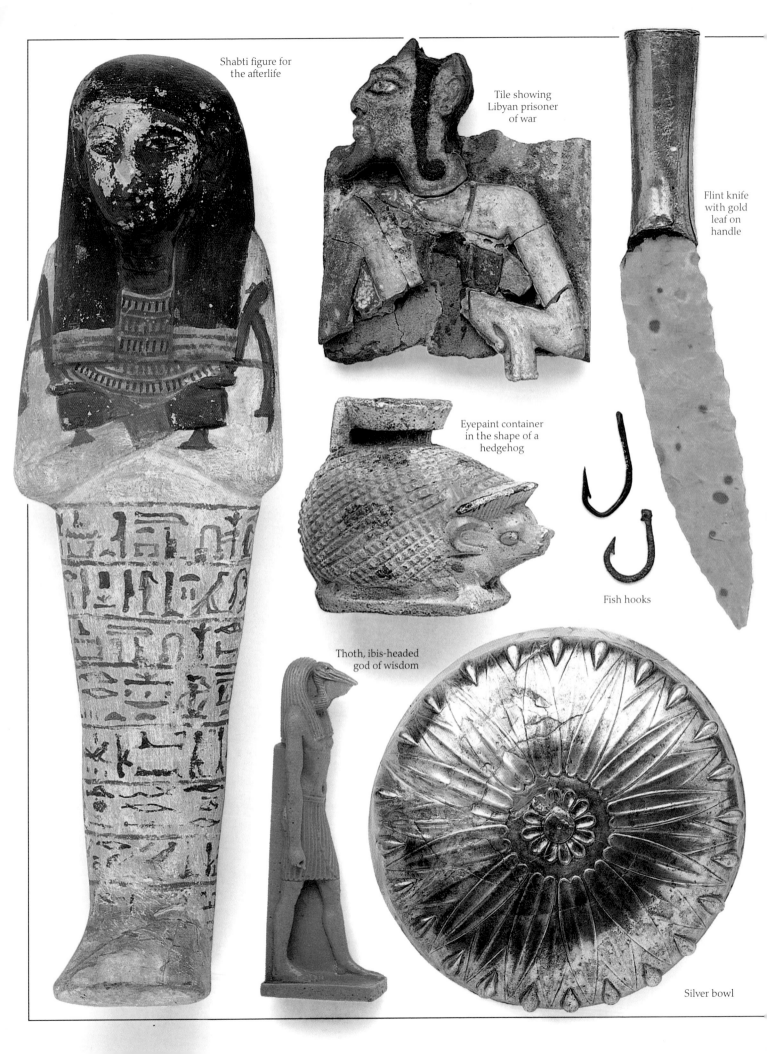

Shabti figure for
the afterlife

Tile showing
Libyan prisoner
of war

Flint knife
with gold
leaf on
handle

Eyepaint container
in the shape of a
hedgehog

Fish hooks

Thoth, ibis-headed
god of wisdom

Silver bowl

Fish amulet
hair pendants

Eyewitness

Gold plaque
showing pharaoh
and sun-god
Atum

ANCIENT EGYPT

Written by
GEORGE HART

Floral inlays
and moulds

Bracelet with
lapis lazuli scarab
set in gold

Paddle doll

Earrings

DK

LONDON, NEW YORK,
MELBOURNE, MUNICH, and DELHI

Wooden
cosmetic
spoon

Project editor Phil Wilkinson
Designer Thomas Keenes
Senior editor Sophie Mitchell
Senior art editor Julia Harris
Editorial director Sue Unstead
Art director Anne-Marie Bulat
Special photography Peter Hayman
of The Department of Egyptian Antiquities,
British Museum

THIS EDITION
Editor Sue Nicholson
Managing editor Camilla Hallinan
Managing art editor Martin Wilson
Publishing manager Sunita Gahir
Category publisher Andrea Pinnington
Production editors Laragh Kedwell,
Andy Hilliard, Hitesh Patel
Production controllers Angela Graef, Pip Tinsley

This Eyewitness ® Guide has been conceived by
Dorling Kindersley Limited and Editions Gallimard

First published in Great Britain in 1990
This revised edition published in 2002, 2007
by Dorling Kindersley Limited,
80 Strand, London WC2R ORL

A CIP catalogue record for this book is
available from the British Library.

ISBN 978-1-40532-153-2

Colour reproduction by Colourscan, Singapore
Printed by Toppan Printing Co., (Shenzhen) Ltd, China

Glass ear studs

Glass tube and
applicator for
eye paint

Discover more at

www.dk.com

Pendant of lapis
lazuli bull's head
set in gold

Contents

Sketch on flake
of limestone

Egypt before the pharaohs

MACEHEAD
This was the kind of weapon used to give the death blow to a wounded enemy. But the smooth surfaces and superb carving of this example make it likely that it was carried by a ruler or high commander on ceremonial occasions.

THE PERIOD we normally think of as "ancient Egypt" is the time when Egypt was ruled by the pharaohs - after c. 3100 BCE. But who lived in Egypt before the pharaohs? In the early Stone Age people in Egypt lived on sites fairly high up on the land above the Nile from the Delta to Aswan. By about 5000 BCE, they had become farmers and began to grow wheat and barley, and to raise and domesticate cattle. They also built villages of mud huts in parts of the flood plain that seemed safe from the annual Nile flood. The farmers prospered and formed kingdoms. Recent excavation shows that by 3,500 BCE, some of them were already living in cities and had made the first steps in inventing writing. They have left behind objects such as magnificently carved ivories and slate palettes, as well as fine pots, often buried with their owners in brick-lined graves.

COMB AND CONCUBINE
The African elephant and hippopotamus provided the early craftsmen with plenty of ivory. The comb is topped by the figure of a gazelle, perhaps because its owner enjoyed hunting this creature. The figure with striking eyes was placed in a tomb and was meant to provide the owner with a female companion in the afterlife.

ANCIENT BODY
Burials at this time, before mummification had evolved, involved arranging the corpse in a "sleeping" position with the elbows and knees drawn together. The body was placed in a pit with a selection of possessions, and sand was thrown on top of it. The sand absorbed all the water from the body, drying it out and preserving it, so that the person's spirit would recognize it and inhabit it. Here you can see the hair and features of a man who died about 5,000 years ago fairly well preserved. When he was found some people thought that he was still lifelike enough to warrant a nickname - Ginger, because of his red hair.

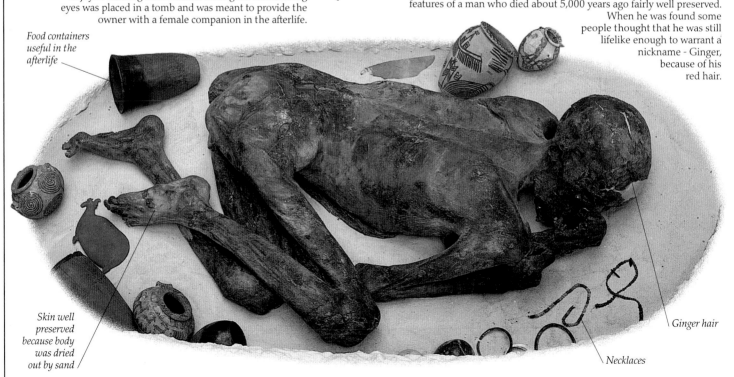

Food containers useful in the afterlife

Skin well preserved because body was dried out by sand

Ginger hair

Necklaces

Carnelian

Feldspar

STONE VASE
This vase was carved from a mottled stone called breccia using simple flint or copper tools. Quartz was used for polishing the surface.

NECKLACES
Early jewellers used semi-precious stones from the deserts. Favourites were feldspar (green) and carnelian (orange). Luxury items like these necklaces show us that before the pharaohs not every labourer was needed to till the soil or hunt for food - craftsmen were already valued members of society and were well rewarded for their skills.

Smooth shape made by simple tools

POTTERY VASE
Nile silt and clay from the edges of the flood plain provided materials for the early potters. This pot's tapering base was designed to fit in a stand or to rest in a depression in the ground. The circular spirals are meant to give the impression of a vessel carved from stone.

Eye inlaid with ivory

Spiral design

COSMETIC PALETTE
Some of the earliest surviving Egyptian objects are slate palettes. They could be rectangular or carved in animal shapes like hippos, turtles, falcons, or this obese ram. The surface was used for grinding minerals for eyepaint (p. 58).

On the banks of the Nile

DESERT COVERS more than 90 per cent of Egypt. Called the "Red Land", the desert supported only small settlements in wadis and oases. The Egyptians lived on the banks of the River Nile or beside canals leading from it. This was "Kemet" or the "Black Land", named after the rich dark silt on which the farmers grew their crops. Without this fertility, there would have been no civilization in Egypt. Right up until modern times the pattern of life in Egypt for the majority of the population has depended on the exploitation of its fertile agricultural resources. Today the population explosion, growth of cities, and the construction of large industrial plants is changing Egyptian lifestyles. The Nile flood began the year for the Egyptian farmer, when the river, increased by the rising waters of the Blue Nile and White Nile converging just north of Khartoum in the Sudan, brought deposits of silt into Egypt. When the Nile waters subsided the farmers got to work sowing barley and emmer wheat. The result was usually a good summer harvest. The High Dam at Aswan, built in the 1960s, totally changed the régime of the river in Egypt.

A RIVERSIDE PEOPLE
The ancient Egyptians lived in a strip of land on either side of the Nile, where the Nile flood made the land fertile. The flood area is shown in green on this map.

River Nile

Red Sea

Desert

FAMINE
In a climate of extremes, crops could sometimes fail and famine could hit the population hard. Statues of people like this beggar remind us of this problem in ancient Egypt.

Herdsman driving cattle with a stick

Scribe with his palette

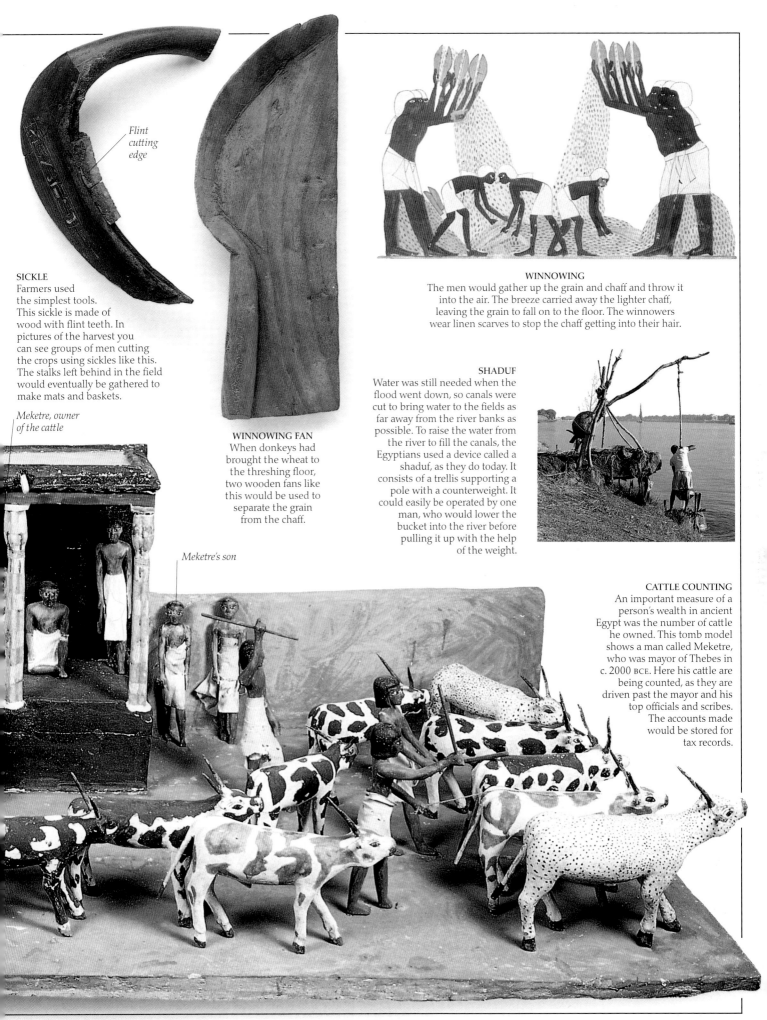

SICKLE
Farmers used the simplest tools. This sickle is made of wood with flint teeth. In pictures of the harvest you can see groups of men cutting the crops using sickles like this. The stalks left behind in the field would eventually be gathered to make mats and baskets.

Flint cutting edge

Meketre, owner of the cattle

WINNOWING FAN
When donkeys had brought the wheat to the threshing floor, two wooden fans like this would be used to separate the grain from the chaff.

Meketre's son

WINNOWING
The men would gather up the grain and chaff and throw it into the air. The breeze carried away the lighter chaff, leaving the grain to fall on to the floor. The winnowers wear linen scarves to stop the chaff getting into their hair.

SHADUF
Water was still needed when the flood went down, so canals were cut to bring water to the fields as far away from the river banks as possible. To raise the water from the river to fill the canals, the Egyptians used a device called a shaduf, as they do today. It consists of a trellis supporting a pole with a counterweight. It could easily be operated by one man, who would lower the bucket into the river before pulling it up with the help of the weight.

CATTLE COUNTING
An important measure of a person's wealth in ancient Egypt was the number of cattle he owned. This tomb model shows a man called Meketre, who was mayor of Thebes in c. 2000 BCE. Here his cattle are being counted, as they are driven past the mayor and his top officials and scribes. The accounts made would be stored for tax records.

Famous pharaohs

The oval enclosing the hieroglyphs that make up a royal name is called a cartouche. This one contains the name of King Tuthmosis III.

THE KING was not only the most powerful and important man in Egypt – he was thought to be a god. He was known as the pharaoh – a word which derives from a respectful way of referring to the king by describing him as the "great house" (per-ao), meaning the palace where he lived. The Queen of Egypt could also be seen as a goddess but was usually given the title of "Great Royal Wife" – only rarely did women rule Egypt in their own right. There was an effective system of training a prince to become a pharaoh, involving him becoming an expert sportsman and potential war leader. Often the ruling pharaoh would adopt his heir as "co-regent" to enable a smooth take-over when he died. Princes sometimes had to wait a long time. One pharaoh holds the record for the longest reign we know for any monarch. Pepy II came to the throne when he was six years old. He was still king of Egypt 94 years later when he was 100. It is quite remarkable in Egypt's long history that we have only a few references to pharaohs being assassinated, usually as a result of a plot in the court to put a prince who was not true heir on to the throne.

ARMLESS QUEEN
This statue shows a queen of Egypt around 700 BCE. Her arms were attached separately but have been lost, as has her crown of plumes.

Osiris, God of the Underworld

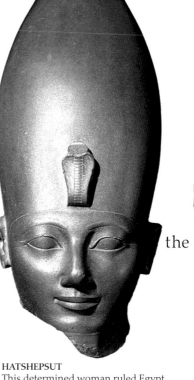

HATSHEPSUT
This determined woman ruled Egypt for about 20 years. She was supposed to be regent for her young stepson, but took over the reins of government. She wore the pharaoh's crown and royal ceremonial beard. In this sculpture she wears the crown of Upper Egypt with the cobra goddess.

Akhenaten

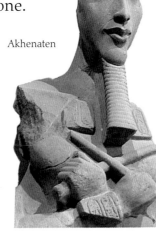

Nefertiti
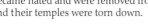

AKHENATEN AND NEFERTITI
In Akhenaten's reign the traditional Egyptian gods were banished - only the sun-god was worshipped. To break the links with other gods, Akhenaten founded a new capital city and closed the temples of other gods. Queen Nefertiti helped her husband set up the cult of the sun-god Aten and probably ruled with him. After their death Tutankhamun and his successors restored the old gods. The names of Akhenaten and Nefertiti became hated and were removed from inscriptions and their temples were torn down.

The mystery of the sphinx

There has been a lot of confusion about sphinxes in ancient Egypt because of Greek legends. In the Greek myth of King Oedipus, the sphinx is a ferocious and lethal female creature who destroys men who are unable to solve the riddle she sets them. But the Egyptians saw the sphinx as a lion's body with the ruler's head. The lion was a creature of the sun-god and so emphasized the king's role as son of Re. The lion's strength also suggests the monarch's great power. Sometimes sphinxes combine other elements such as the head and wings of a hawk symbolizing the god Horus.

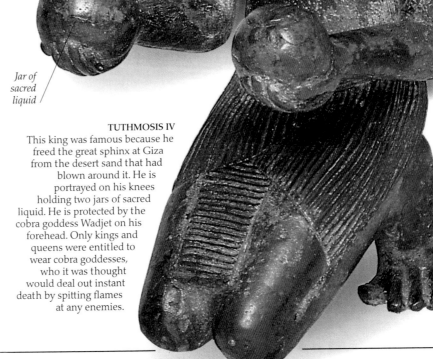

SPHINX AT GIZA
This sphinx was carved around 4,500 years ago for the pharaoh Khafre and guarded the way to his pyramid.

SPHINX AND PRISONER
The way that the sphinx represents the pharaoh's power is shown in this ivory statuette, carved over 3,600 years ago.

RAMESSES THE GREAT
In the 13th century BCE, Ramesses II reigned over Egypt for 67 years. He built more monuments and set up more statues than any other pharaoh. Among his buildings are the mortuary complex on the West Bank at Thebes, today called the Ramesseum, from which this statue comes. The king wears a royal headcloth called the "nemes", above which is a crown of cobras.

Ceremonial beard

Cobra goddess

Head cloth

Jar of sacred liquid

TUTANKHAMUN
This ruler came to the throne at only nine years old. He was obviously guided by his high officials, but seems to have been determined to bring back the old gods who had been banished by Akhenaten (see left). This famous golden mask comes from his tomb (p. 23).

TUTHMOSIS IV
This king was famous because he freed the great sphinx at Giza from the desert sand that had blown around it. He is portrayed on his knees holding two jars of sacred liquid. He is protected by the cobra goddess Wadjet on his forehead. Only kings and queens were entitled to wear cobra goddesses, who it was thought would deal out instant death by spitting flames at any enemies.

The royal court

ROYAL HEAD
This portrait in glass was probably used as an inlay in a piece of palace furniture or as a decoration around a window.

AT GREAT STATE OCCASIONS like royal jubilee celebrations or the giving of gifts to favoured courtiers, the king and court gathered together, and top officials, diplomats, and high priests would attend. Some of these courtiers were relatives of the king, some won high office through their ability as scribes. When people approached the king, they often kissed the ground beneath his feet. We know this because one courtier boasted that the pharaoh insisted that he kiss the royal leg and not the ground. Sometimes the pharaoh simply wanted to relax at court.

King Sneferu was all set to watch 20 beautiful women of his harem row on the royal lake. It went well until one girl dropped her hair clasp in the lake, began to sulk, and stopped rowing; she refused even the king's request to carry on. The court magician had to part the waters and get the clasp from the bottom.

Lion's-paw legs

ROYAL THRONE
Queen Hetepheres was the mother of King Khufu (p. 20). Her original burial place was robbed but some of her splendid furniture was reburied near her son's pyramid. The court throne was made of wood overlaid with gold leaf. Insects ate the wood away but archaeologists were able to reconstruct the furniture.

FISHES
Children sometimes wore fish-shaped amulets in their hair, possibly to guard against accidents in the Nile.

OYSTER-SHELL PENDANT
The earliest jewellery in Egypt was often made of shells. Later jewellers imitated these shapes in gold. This one is carved with the name of King Senwosret.

AMULET CASE
Protective spells (written on papyrus) or amulets could be put in a container like this and hung from a necklace.

CEREMONIAL THROWSTICK
Courtiers used wooden throwsticks to catch birds. This one, made of brittle faience (p. 47), would have no practical use - it was intended to be carried during ceremonies. It bears the name of Akhenaten, the pharaoh who lived in the 14th century BCE.

ROYAL VASES
The pharaohs used the best quality utensils and cosmetic containers, which were buried in their tombs for use in the next world. These two smoothly carved mottled stone vases have lids of gold adorned with imitation twine, also in gold. They were made for King Khasekhemwy.

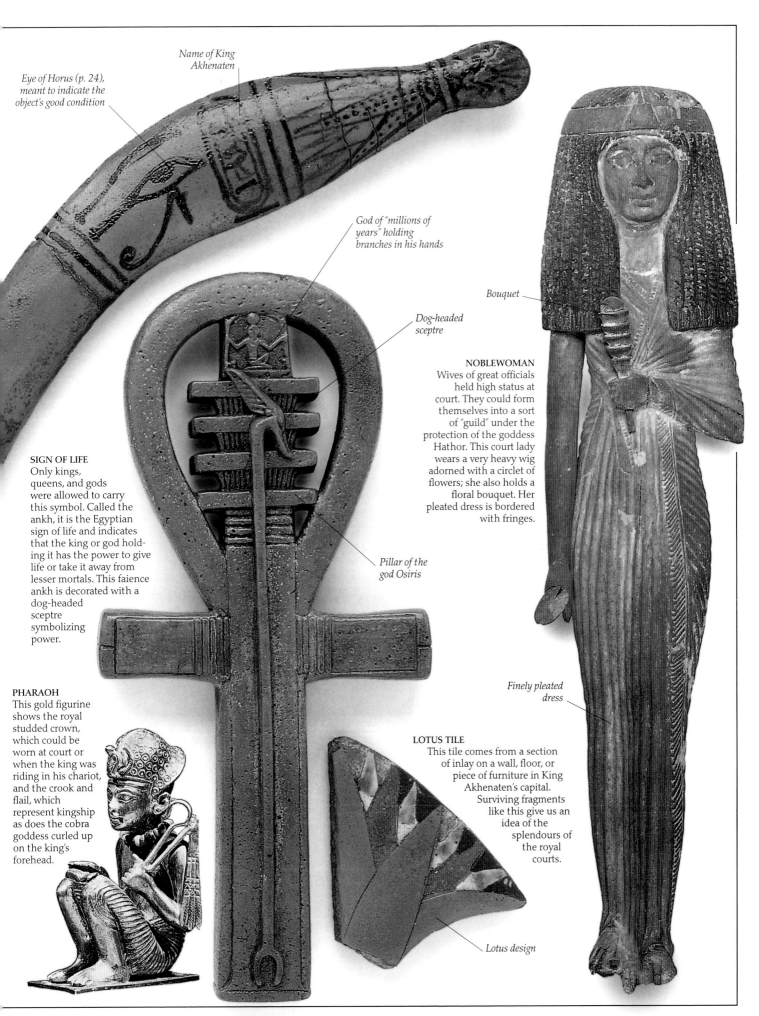

Eye of Horus (p. 24), meant to indicate the object's good condition

Name of King Akhenaten

God of "millions of years" holding branches in his hands

Dog-headed sceptre

Bouquet

SIGN OF LIFE
Only kings, queens, and gods were allowed to carry this symbol. Called the ankh, it is the Egyptian sign of life and indicates that the king or god holding it has the power to give life or take it away from lesser mortals. This faience ankh is decorated with a dog-headed sceptre symbolizing power.

Pillar of the god Osiris

NOBLEWOMAN
Wives of great officials held high status at court. They could form themselves into a sort of "guild" under the protection of the goddess Hathor. This court lady wears a very heavy wig adorned with a circlet of flowers; she also holds a floral bouquet. Her pleated dress is bordered with fringes.

Finely pleated dress

PHARAOH
This gold figurine shows the royal studded crown, which could be worn at court or when the king was riding in his chariot, and the crook and flail, which represent kingship as does the cobra goddess curled up on the king's forehead.

LOTUS TILE
This tile comes from a section of inlay on a wall, floor, or piece of furniture in King Akhenaten's capital. Surviving fragments like this give us an idea of the splendours of the royal courts.

Lotus design

13

Preparing for the tomb

THE EGYPTIANS dreaded the thought that one day their world might cease to exist. With their belief in the power of magic, they developed a funerary cult which, in their eyes, ensured their survival for ever. This involved preserving the body of the deceased. The embalmers took the body to the Beautiful House, where they worked. They made a cut in the left side of the body with a flint knife and removed the liver and lungs. These were dried out and stored in special vessels called "canopic jars". The brain was also removed, but the heart was left in the body, so that it could be weighed in the afterlife (p. 19). Then the body was covered with crystals of a substance called natron, which stopped it rotting, packed with dry material like leaves or sawdust, and wrapped in linen bandages.

This scarab was placed over the heart of a king to help him through the scrutiny of his past life that happened in the underworld.

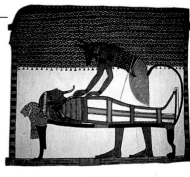

ANUBIS
The god Anubis was supposed to be responsible for the ritual of embalming. His titles included "He who is in the place of embalming". Here he is putting the final touches to a mummified corpse.

Instrument for touching the mouth

Vase

WAX PLATE
Plates like this were used to cover cuts made in the flesh of the corpse. The protective eye of Horus (p. 24), symbolized the soundness of the body on which it was placed.

UTENSILS FOR "OPENING THE MOUTH"
One of the most important of all funerary rites, this ceremony restored a dead person's living faculties, allowing the mummy to eat, drink, and move around. Egyptians hated to die abroad because they knew that their corpse would not receive this rite and their afterlife would be in jeopardy. This model kit contains some of the instruments for the "Opening the mouth" ceremony. There are vases for the sacred liquids, cups for pouring libations, and a forked instrument for touching the mouth of the mummy.

OPENING THE MOUTH
A priest wearing the mask of Anubis holds the coffin upright. Behind the grieving wife and daughter, priests scatter purified water and touch the mouth of the mummy case with the ritual instruments. The eldest son burns incense and a spell is recited.

CANOPIC JARS
Any part of your body could be used in a spell against you, so the inner organs removed during mummification were protected by special containers called canopic jars. Dried out and wrapped up in linen, the intestines, stomach, liver, and lungs were each placed in a separate jar.

MUMMY LABELS
Small wooden dockets attached to mummies identified the body and gave protection. On one of these Anubis is shown. He is black because this is the colour of life in ancient Egypt, being the colour of the fertile Nile mud, but it is also the colour of mummified bodies.

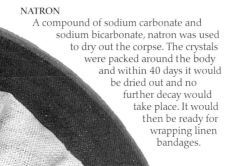

WHAT'S INSIDE?
An X-ray of a mummy reveals the stuffing that replaced some of its organs.

NATRON
A compound of sodium carbonate and sodium bicarbonate, natron was used to dry out the corpse. The crystals were packed around the body and within 40 days it would be dried out and no further decay would take place. It would then be ready for wrapping linen bandages.

Ancient linen wrapping

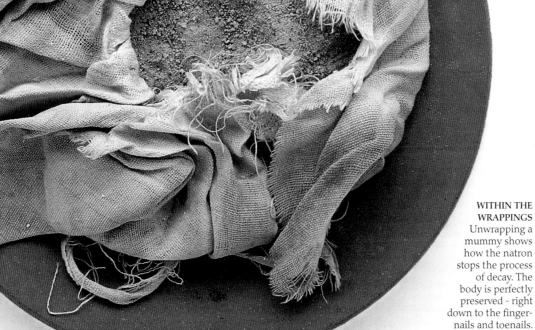

WITHIN THE WRAPPINGS
Unwrapping a mummy shows how the natron stops the process of decay. The body is perfectly preserved - right down to the fingernails and toenails.

Everlasting bodies

THE FINAL STAGE in the embalming process was to put the body into its coffin. For a rich person, this could be an elaborate container made up of several different, richly decorated layers. The body would then be well preserved and, as far as the Egyptians were concerned, would last for ever. The reason they did this was that they thought that after a person's physical death a number of elements lived on. The most important was a person's "Ka", which they thought of as the body's double and which could bring the corpse back to life. Another spirit that survived was a person's "Ba", which had the head of the deceased and the body of a hawk. They also thought that a person's shadow had an eternal existence as well as their name. The process of mummification was intended to make an everlasting body out of a corpse that was ready to decompose, and to provide the Ka with a home in the afterlife. The superbly preserved bodies that have been found in Egyptian tombs show how successful the embalmers were.

HORROR HERO
The body of Ramesses III, who ruled over Egypt in the 12th century BCE, shows his eyes packed with linen and his arms still positioned as if holding the crook and flail sceptres (p. 13). Actor Boris Karloff had his mummy costume and features modelled on Ramesses III for his role in the film *The Mummy*.

Hand and arm from Egyptian mummy, showing details of skin and nails

MUMMY CASE
Wrapped in linen bandages, the body was free from decay and the family would not be able to see any mistakes the embalmers might have made - there are examples of a head that snapped off being fixed on to the neck with a stick, and a queen whose face was so well stuffed with pads of linen that it broke away from the rest of her head. The interior of the coffin could be richly decorated with gods of the underworld, while the outside could be ablaze with colourful hieroglyphs of spells destined to help the dead person in the the kingdom of Osiris.

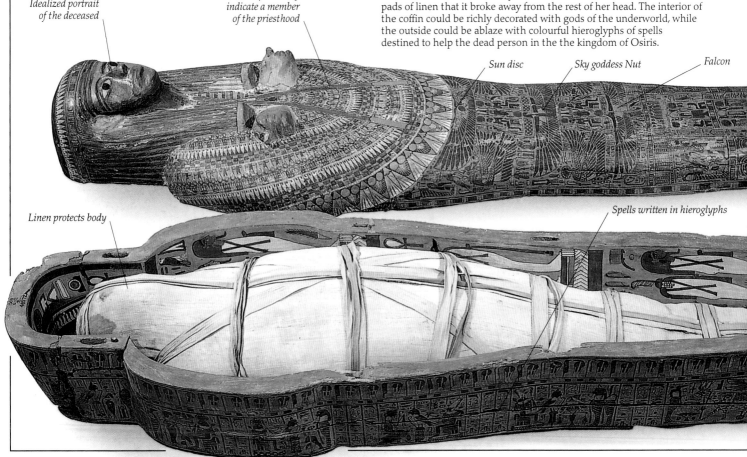

Idealized portrait of the deceased

Red straps usually indicate a member of the priesthood

Sun disc

Sky goddess Nut

Falcon

Linen protects body

Spells written in hieroglyphs

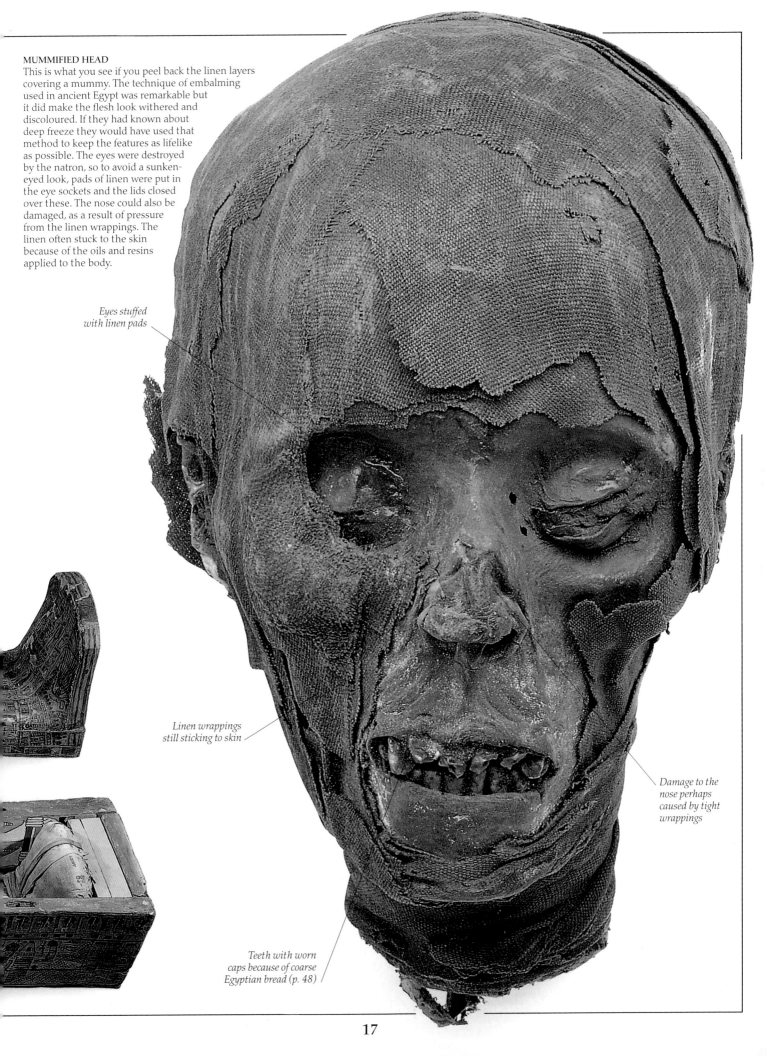

MUMMIFIED HEAD
This is what you see if you peel back the linen layers covering a mummy. The technique of embalming used in ancient Egypt was remarkable but it did make the flesh look withered and discoloured. If they had known about deep freeze they would have used that method to keep the features as lifelike as possible. The eyes were destroyed by the natron, so to avoid a sunken-eyed look, pads of linen were put in the eye sockets and the lids closed over these. The nose could also be damaged, as a result of pressure from the linen wrappings. The linen often stuck to the skin because of the oils and resins applied to the body.

Eyes stuffed with linen pads

Linen wrappings still sticking to skin

Damage to the nose perhaps caused by tight wrappings

Teeth with worn caps because of coarse Egyptian bread (p. 48)

Journey to the afterlife

Outspread arms show the god's power extended beyond its own body

BELOW THE EARTH the ancient Egyptians imagined there existed an underworld which they called Duat. Some parts of it were full of perils like lakes of fire, poisonous snakes, and executioners. Spells were used to counteract these dangers. Many of them were written on coffins, together with a map of the underworld. These developed into ornate scrolls of papyrus which we call Books of the Dead, since many were discovered on or near mummies. The book was a passport through all the perils lurking in Duat. If you could recite the correct spells, you could pass through unharmed. The ultimate danger was to fail the test set for you in the Hall of the Two Truths, where your heart was weighed against your past deeds. The papyrus helped you as much as possible to pass the examination and reach a land that was just like Egypt itself.

HIRED MOURNERS
The more mourners at a funeral the higher the status of the deceased. As well as the family, women were hired to mourn at funerals. They would wave their arms, throw dust over their hair, and weep.

Ram-headed god statue covered in black resin

RAM-HEADED GOD
Sometimes statues of underworld gods were taken into the tombs in the Valley of the Kings (p. 22). With their power to ward off evil, they were meant to protect the king as he travelled through the underworld. These gods had heads of creatures such as tortoises, hippos, or rams. They are quite different from other animal-headed deities (p. 24), who flourished above ground.

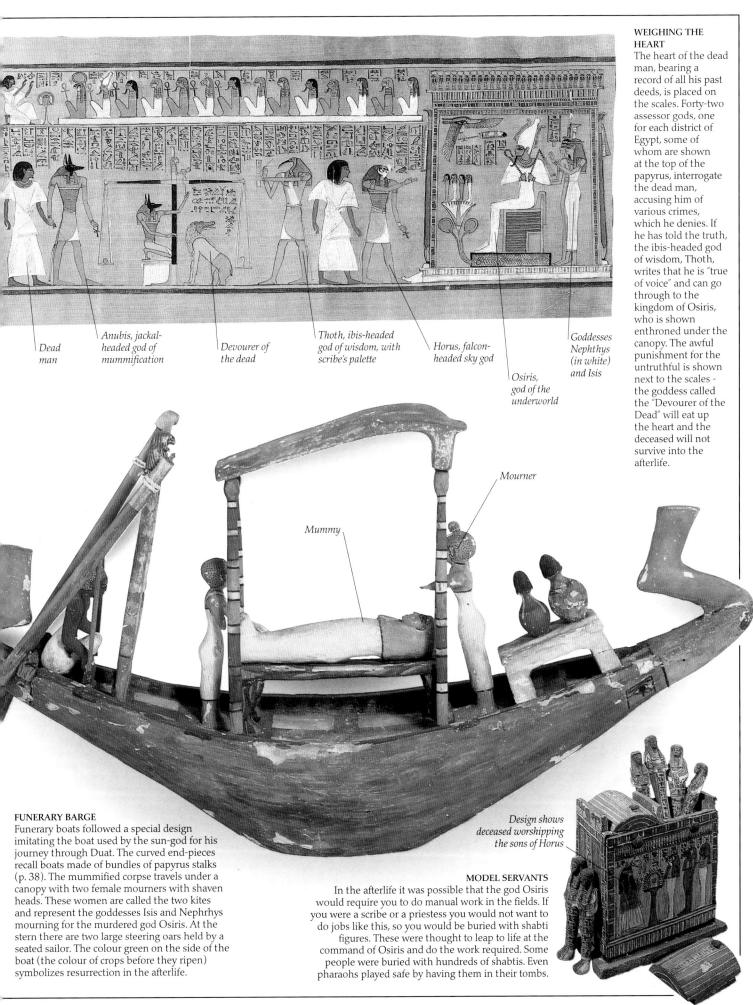

The heart of the dead man, bearing a record of all his past deeds, is placed on the scales. Forty-two assessor gods, one for each district of Egypt, some of whom are shown at the top of the papyrus, interrogate the dead man, accusing him of various crimes, which he denies. If he has told the truth, the ibis-headed god of wisdom, Thoth, writes that he is "true of voice" and can go through to the kingdom of Osiris, who is shown enthroned under the canopy. The awful punishment for the untruthful is shown next to the scales - the goddess called the "Devourer of the Dead" will eat up the heart and the deceased will not survive into the afterlife.

Dead man

Anubis, jackal-headed god of mummification

Devourer of the dead

Thoth, ibis-headed god of wisdom, with scribe's palette

Horus, falcon-headed sky god

Osiris, god of the underworld

Goddesses Nephthys (in white) and Isis

Mummy

Mourner

Design shows deceased worshipping the sons of Horus

FUNERARY BARGE

Funerary boats followed a special design imitating the boat used by the sun-god for his journey through Duat. The curved end-pieces recall boats made of bundles of papyrus stalks (p. 38). The mummified corpse travels under a canopy with two female mourners with shaven heads. These women are called the two kites and represent the goddesses Isis and Nephrhys mourning for the murdered god Osiris. At the stern there are two large steering oars held by a seated sailor. The colour green on the side of the boat (the colour of crops before they ripen) symbolizes resurrection in the afterlife.

MODEL SERVANTS

In the afterlife it was possible that the god Osiris would require you to do manual work in the fields. If you were a scribe or a priestess you would not want to do jobs like this, so you would be buried with shabti figures. These were thought to leap to life at the command of Osiris and do the work required. Some people were buried with hundreds of shabtis. Even pharaohs played safe by having them in their tombs.

The great pyramids

THE FIRST PYRAMID was built as the burial place of King Djoser in c. 2650 BCE, by his gifted architect Imhotep (pp. 34-35). It rose in six stages and is called the Step Pyramid. It was supposed to represent a gigantic stairway for the king to climb to join the sun-god in the sky. Some later kings had step pyramids too, but in the reign of King Sneferu the true pyramid with sloping sides developed. The idea of this pyramid was to recreate the mound that had emerged out of the watery ground at the beginning of time, on which the sun-god stood and brought the other gods and goddesses into being. The largest pyramid of all is the Great Pyramid at Giza, built for King Khufu in c. 2589 BCE. The pyramids were intended to protect the bodies of the pharaohs buried deep inside them. Later pyramids contained inscriptions of spells to help the pharoah in the afterlife. Doors of granite and false passages were constructed to deter robbers who came in pursuit of the rich offerings buried with the kings. But by c. 1000 BCE all the pyramids had been robbed of their precious contents.

GRAND GALLERY
This gallery, 47 m (154 ft) long and 8.5 m (28 ft) high, rises towards the burial chamber. It has a magnificent stone roof. After the burial, great blocks of granite were slid down the gallery to seal off the burial chamber. The pharaoh's sarcophagus could not have been pulled up the gallery into the burial chamber – it is wider than the gallery and must have been constructed when the pyramid was being built.

CLIMBERS
Today there is a law in Egypt forbidding visitors from climbing the Great Pyramid. But in the 19th century many people felt the urge to climb the pyramid and admire the view below. It was not difficult to climb, but if you slipped it was almost impossible to regain your footing.

Small pyramids, the burial places of the three chief wives of Khufu

Mortuary temple, where offerings could be made

THE GREAT PYRAMID
Built for King Khufu around 4,500 years ago, the Great Pyramid was one of the seven Wonders of the World. It contains over 2.3 million limestone blocks ranging from 2.5 to 15 tonnes in weight. The builders may have had levers to help get the stones into place, but had no pulleys or other machinery. The whole pyramid probably took about 20 years to build. There was a standing workforce of craftsmen and labourers, which was swelled every year for three months when the Nile flooded and the field workers were sent on national service to help on the construction work. The pyramids were just one part of the funerary complex devoted to the pharaoh's afterlife. There would also be a mortuary temple for cult offering and a causeway leading to the valley temple - the place where the King's body was received after its last journey along the river Nile.

Causeway connecting pyramid to temple in Nile valley

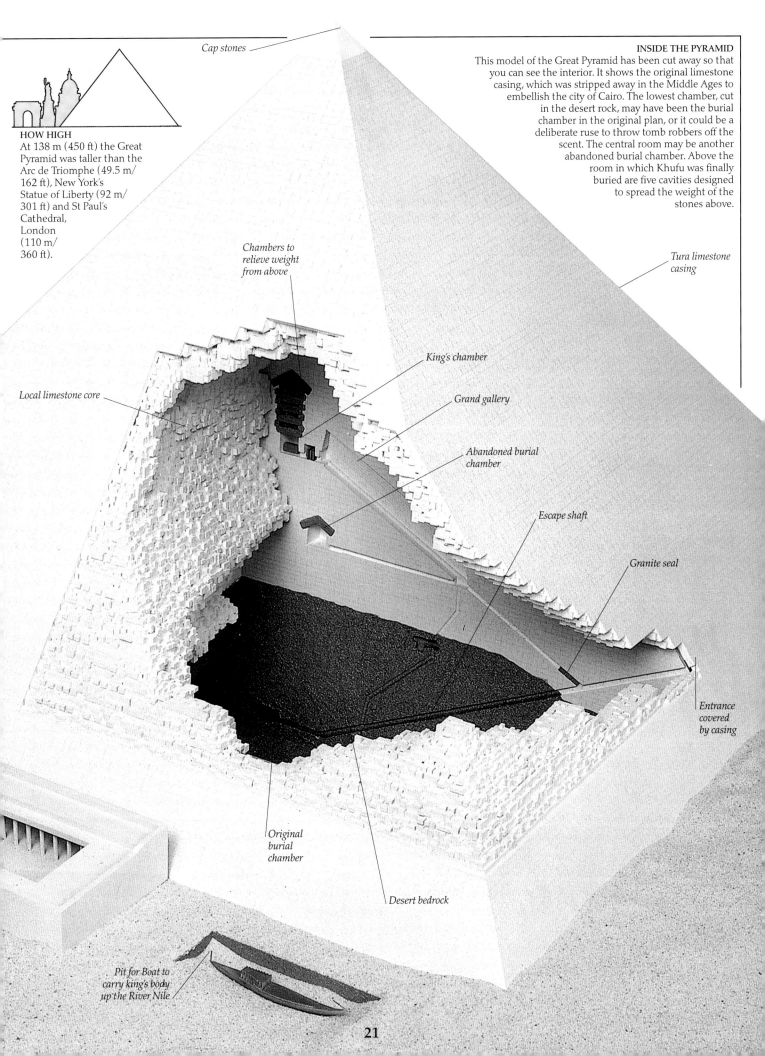

Cap stones

This model of the Great Pyramid has been cut away so that you can see the interior. It shows the original limestone casing, which was stripped away in the Middle Ages to embellish the city of Cairo. The lowest chamber, cut in the desert rock, may have been the burial chamber in the original plan, or it could be a deliberate ruse to throw tomb robbers off the scent. The central room may be another abandoned burial chamber. Above the room in which Khufu was finally buried are five cavities designed to spread the weight of the stones above.

HOW HIGH
At 138 m (450 ft) the Great Pyramid was taller than the Arc de Triomphe (49.5 m/ 162 ft), New York's Statue of Liberty (92 m/ 301 ft) and St Paul's Cathedral, London (110 m/ 360 ft).

Chambers to relieve weight from above

King's chamber

Grand gallery

Abandoned burial chamber

Local limestone core

Escape shaft

Granite seal

Tura limestone casing

Entrance covered by casing

Original burial chamber

Desert bedrock

Pit for Boat to carry king's body up the River Nile

The Valley of the Kings

RAMESSES VI
This king, who died in 1136 BCE, was buried in a granite coffin that weighed many tonnes. This is part of the lid.

THE PYRAMID AGE drew to a close in c. 2150 BCE. Nearly all the pharaohs from Tuthmosis I (1504 BCE) to Ramesses XI (1070 BCE) chose to be buried in tombs in the Valley of the Kings. Remote from the flood plain, the valley lay deep in the cliffs to the west of the Nile. There was a ridge in front of the entrance where guards were posted. Some of the tombs were placed high in the cliff side in an attempt to conceal their entrances from robbers; others had elaborate portals and were much more obvious. The usual pattern was for the tomb to have a deep corridor - known as the "Way of the Sun-God" - with a well or shaft near the inner end that was intended to catch rainwater and to deter tomb robbers. Beyond this was the "Hall of Gold", where the king would be buried. He would be surrounded by gilded furniture and jewellery, royal clothing, and regalia. The contents of the tomb of Tutankhamun were the only ones to escape the hands of the robbers before c. 1000 BCE.

UNDERWORLD DEITY
This hippopotamus-headed god was found in the tomb of Tuthmosis III. It is covered in a black resin - black was the colour of life in ancient Egypt. It looks ferocious, but its anger is directed only at the king's enemies. It probably represented one of the guardians of the secret portals of the mansion of the god Osiris.

SACRED SERPENT
The Valley was thought to be protected by a goddess, called Meretseger, who was portrayed as a cobra. The tomb workers thought she would blind or poison criminals or those who swore false oaths.

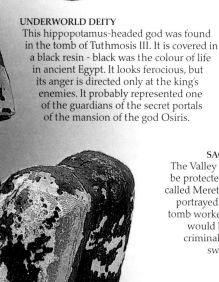

VALLEY VIEW
This view of the Valley of the Kings by the 19th century artist David Roberts conveys something of the solitude of the place. Today it is much busier, with a modern road, coach park, and the stalls of souvenir sellers destroying the ancient atmosphere.

UNKNOWN KING
This king's statue was found in the tomb of Tutankhamun, but no one knows why it was buried there. The monarch wears the Red Crown, showing authority over Lower Egypt. His crook stands for kingship, his flail for the fertility of the land.

DEIR EL MEDINA
These stone foundations are all that is left of the village where the workers on the tombs lived. Founded in the 16th century BCE, it flourished for 500 years - as long as the kings continued to be buried in the valley. Usually about 60 families lived in these houses.

Tutankhamun's tomb

The resting place of the young king Tutankhamun was the only tomb of a New Kingdom pharaoh to escape almost untouched by robbers. It was the last of the valley tombs to be discovered, being found by Howard Carter in 1922. Its contents included weapons, clothes, furniture, jewellery, musical instruments, and model boats, as well as the king's famous coffins and mask (p. 11). Many of these items were either made of solid gold or were richly decorated with gold leaf. The king was buried with his two still-born daughters and a treasured heirloom - a lock of hair of his grandmother Queen Tiye.

ALL DRESSED UP
The delicate items discovered in Tutankhamun's tomb had to be carefully prepared for transport to Cairo Museum. Archaeologists Howard Carter and Lord Caernarvon are here wrapping up one of the guardian statues from the tomb.

Gods and goddesses

THE EGYPTIANS worshipped hundreds of different gods and goddesses, and sometimes it is difficult to work out who was who. Many of the gods are represented by animals: a baboon might stand for Thoth, god of wisdom, at one temple, and a moon-god called Khonsu at another. Each of the 42 different administrative districts (or "nomes") had its own god, and there were many others besides. Overall the sun-god was the dominant deity in Egyptian religion, although he could take different forms. At dawn he would be Khepri, the scarab beetle rolling the sun disc above the eastern horizon. In the evening the god was Atum, an old man. He could become Re-Harakhty, the great hawk soaring in the sky. He was seen as responsible for all creation - people, animals, the fertility of the soil, and the king's journey through the underworld. As Amun-Re he was king of the gods and protector of the pharaoh when he went on military campaigns. The pharaoh Akhenaten saw the sun-god as a disc with rays ending in human hands holding the sign of life to the royal family, and he banished all other gods. His son Tutankhamun restored them once more (pp10–11).

THE GODS AND THEIR MAKERS
This detail from a 19th-century painting shows the artist's idea of a workshop in which Egyptian figures of the gods were made. The cat is modelling for an image of Bastet (opposite).

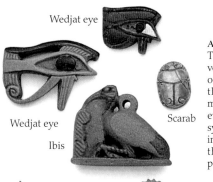

Wedjat eye

Wedjat eye

Ibis

Scarab

Winged scarab

AMULETS
The "wedjat" eye symbolizes both the vengeful eye of the sun god and the eye of the god Horus, torn out by Seth in the struggle for the throne of Egypt, but magically restored. It was said to protect everything behind it. The scarab beetle symbolized the sun-god Khepri. The real insect pushes a ball of dung around, and the Egyptians imagined that the sun was propelled in a similar way. The sacred ibis represents Thoth, god of wisdom and healing.

AMUN-RE *right*
Amun-Re became the principal god during the New Kindgom. He handed the scimitar of conquest to the great warrior pharaohs like Tuthmosis III. He has a mysterious nature, which even the other gods were unaware of - the word "Amun" means "hidden".

THOTH *below*
The curved beak of the ibis was like the crescent moon, so the bird became the symbol of the moon god Thoth. He gave the Egyptians knowledge of writing, medicine, and mathematics, and was the patron of the scribes.

ANUBIS
Jackals used to haunt cemeteries, so they were linked with funerals - the idea being that a jackal god would protect the domain of the dead. Anubis also supervised embalming (p. 14) and looked after the place where mummification was done.

GODS OF PROSPERITY
These figures are tying together lotus and papyrus, the plants of Upper and Lower Egypt, around the hieroglyph meaning "unite". Often called the "Nile gods", these figures were symbols of the fertility that came from the river's annual flood.

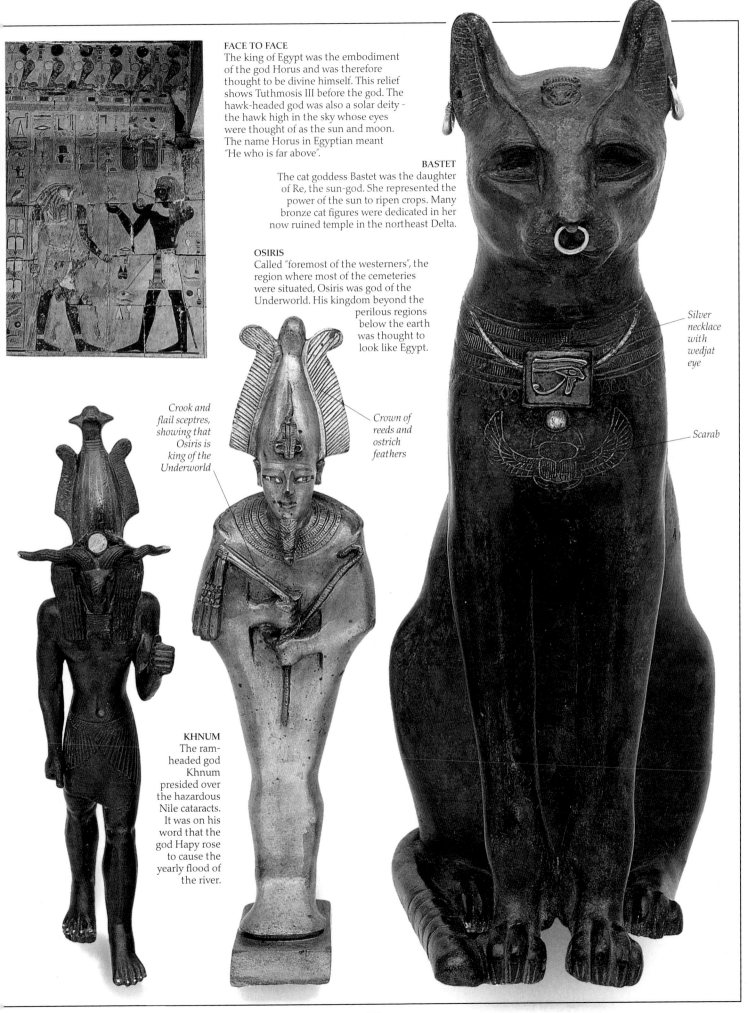

FACE TO FACE
The king of Egypt was the embodiment of the god Horus and was therefore thought to be divine himself. This relief shows Tuthmosis III before the god. The hawk-headed god was also a solar deity - the hawk high in the sky whose eyes were thought of as the sun and moon. The name Horus in Egyptian meant "He who is far above".

BASTET
The cat goddess Bastet was the daughter of Re, the sun-god. She represented the power of the sun to ripen crops. Many bronze cat figures were dedicated in her now ruined temple in the northeast Delta.

OSIRIS
Called "foremost of the westerners", the region where most of the cemeteries were situated, Osiris was god of the Underworld. His kingdom beyond the perilous regions below the earth was thought to look like Egypt.

Silver necklace with wedjat eye

Scarab

Crook and flail sceptres, showing that Osiris is king of the Underworld

Crown of reeds and ostrich feathers

KHNUM
The ram-headed god Khnum presided over the hazardous Nile cataracts. It was on his word that the god Hapy rose to cause the yearly flood of the river.

Magic and medicine

Headrest amulet

THE GODS OF THE TEMPLES played little part in the lives of ancient Egyptians, so people turned to magic to ease problems like the dangers of childbirth, infant mortality, and fevers. The Egyptians also had great medical skills. Physicians' papyrus manuals survive which describe how to treat ailments and reveal a detailed knowledge of anatomy. They wrote about the importance of the heart and how it "speaks out" through the back of the head and hands - a reference to the pulse beat. There were remedies for eye disorders, tumours, and gynaecological complaints. The Egyptians believed that many diseases came from worm-like creatures invading the body. Physicians and magicians worked together, using both medicines and spells for problems like snake bites or scorpion stings. They also used magic to ward off possible injuries from crocodiles or the ghosts of the dead. Letters to the dead could be written on pottery bowls and put in tombs if a person felt that a dead relative's spirit was upset or likely to cause trouble. Dangers were also counteracted by amulets or magical charms.

Panel from the tomb of Hesire, the king's dentist in c. 2700 BCE.

AMULETS
Magical charms could be worn on necklaces and bracelets while a person was alive, and placed on the corpse in the mummy wrappings to give protection in the next life. They were supposed to ward off any injury and were sometimes accompanied by spells.

Pillar amulet

Knot amulet

Powerful plants

Plants played an important part in both magic and medicine. Many were very valuable - juniper berries were thought to be important enough for them to be imported from Lebanon. Others, like garlic, were used for medicinal properties still valued in some parts of the world today, but were used in magic too.

LOTUS
This flower was very important to the Egyptians - they decorated their temples and many of their belongings with images of the lotus.

Lotus blossom

JUNIPER BERRIES
These were placed in the mummies of royalty, courtiers, or crocodiles, or left in baskets in tombs. Their juice was used in the purification rituals performed over the corpse.

GARLIC
This plant was used in burials. It was also thought to repel snakes and expel tapeworms.

HENNA
Used to colour the hair and skin, henna was supposed to have the power to ward off danger.

HEAR OUR PRAYER
This stela contains a prayer to the god Ptah, surrounded by ears to help him hear it.

GODDESS OF CHILDBIRTH
Prayers to this goddess were an essential part of giving birth. She was called Taweret, and is shown as a pregnant hippopotamus. She can look ferocious - this is to keep away evil from attacking the woman as she gives birth. Magic liquid could be poured out of her breast.

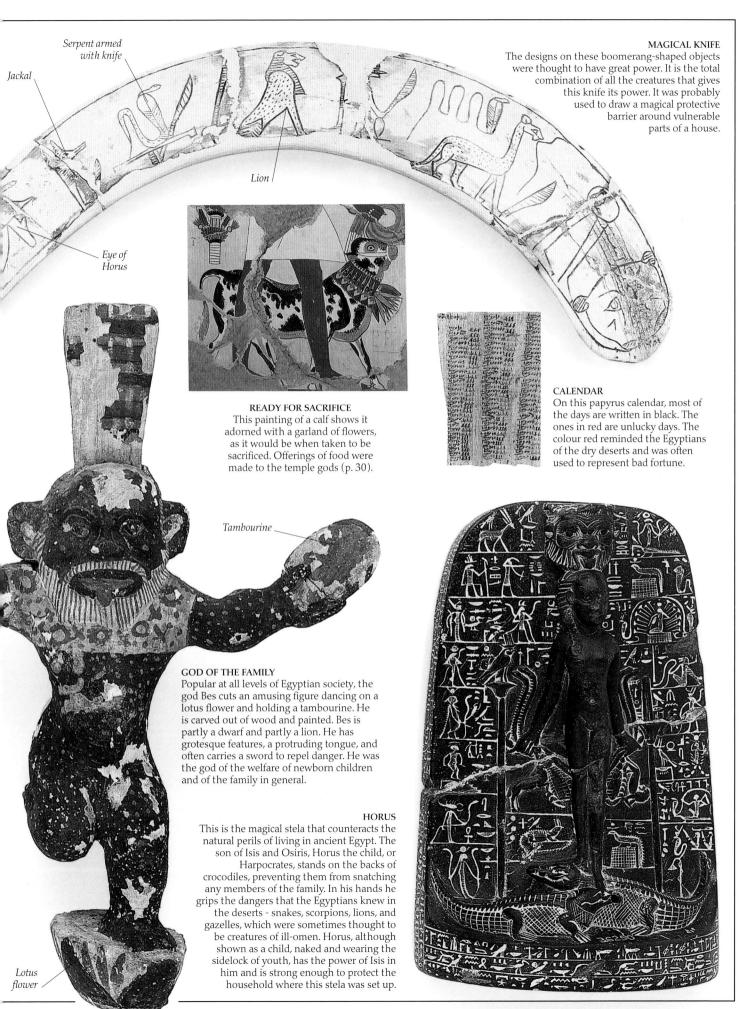

Serpent armed
with knife

Jackal

MAGICAL KNIFE
The designs on these boomerang-shaped objects
were thought to have great power. It is the total
combination of all the creatures that gives
this knife its power. It was probably
used to draw a magical protective
barrier around vulnerable
parts of a house.

Lion

Eye of
Horus

READY FOR SACRIFICE
This painting of a calf shows it
adorned with a garland of flowers,
as it would be when taken to be
sacrificed. Offerings of food were
made to the temple gods (p. 30).

CALENDAR
On this papyrus calendar, most of
the days are written in black. The
ones in red are unlucky days. The
colour red reminded the Egyptians
of the dry deserts and was often
used to represent bad fortune.

Tambourine

GOD OF THE FAMILY
Popular at all levels of Egyptian society, the
god Bes cuts an amusing figure dancing on a
lotus flower and holding a tambourine. He
is carved out of wood and painted. Bes is
partly a dwarf and partly a lion. He has
grotesque features, a protruding tongue, and
often carries a sword to repel danger. He was
the god of the welfare of newborn children
and of the family in general.

HORUS
This is the magical stela that counteracts the
natural perils of living in ancient Egypt. The
son of Isis and Osiris, Horus the child, or
Harpocrates, stands on the backs of
crocodiles, preventing them from snatching
any members of the family. In his hands he
grips the dangers that the Egyptians knew in
the deserts - snakes, scorpions, lions, and
gazelles, which were sometimes thought to
be creatures of ill-omen. Horus, although
shown as a child, naked and wearing the
sidelock of youth, has the power of Isis in
him and is strong enough to protect the
household where this stela was set up.

Lotus
flower

Priests and temples

I N THEORY, the pharaoh was supposed to carry out the duties of the high priest in every temple in Egypt, but his place was usually taken by the chief priest. In the great temples such as Karnak at Thebes, sacred to Amun-Re, King of the Gods, the chief priest had great power and controlled the vast wealth in the temple treasuries and the great lands of the temple estates. The office of chief priest could remain in the hands of one family for generations until the pharaoh broke their hold by making an appointment from outside. The priests had titles to indicate their power - they could be called "God's Servant", with the addition of "First", "Second", or "Third", to show their position. Priests at lower levels could be called "Pure Ones" or "God's Fathers" and would have the responsibility of serving on the temple rota system, maintaining the temple's property, and keeping administrative records.

FEED THE BIRDS
Sacred to the god Thoth, ibises were revered in Egypt. This detail from a fanciful 19th century painting shows ibises being fed by a priestess.

Sidelock of hair

KNEELING PRIEST
This type of priest was called a "Yun-mutef" priest, meaning "Pillar of his Mother". He symbolizes the divine child Horus (p. 27), wears a leopardskin, and has his hair in a sidelock to represent youth. He kneels at an offering table.

Offering table

Paw and tail of leopardskin

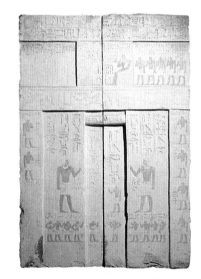

FALSE DOOR
Courtiers had tomb chapels with false doors, which stood for the idea of contact between the tomb and the place where offerings to the gods could be made. "Soul priests" would leave offerings of food and drink at these doors - on this door several bearers are shown bringing meat, poultry, and bread to the tomb.

THE TEMPLE OF DENDERA
The goddess Hathor's temple as it survives today belongs to the time when Egypt was ruled by the Greeks and Romans (pp. 62-63) - in fact Queen Cleopatra is shown on its rear wall. The heads belong to the goddess Hathor.

LAST OF THE TEMPLES
This detail of a painting by David Roberts, who travelled widely in Egypt in the 19th century, shows the temple of Isis on the island of Philae. This was the final Egyptian temple to fall to the Christians. The Roman emperor Justinian closed it in the 6th century CE, and ordered it to be turned into a church.

COLOSSAL CARVINGS
Near the second cataract of the Nile at Abu Simbel in Nubia, Ramesses II ordered two temples to be carved out of the sandstone cliffs. This one was carved for himself and three major Egyptian gods - Amun, Re-Harakhty, and Ptah. Huge statues of Ramesses flank the entrance.

Obelisks

The Egyptians carved stone obelisks with the titles of their kings and dedications to the gods. The pointed tip of the obelisk represents the ground on which the sun-god stood to create the universe.

GATEPOST?
This obelisk was one of two that stood at the entrance to the temple at Luxor. The other obelisk was given to the king of France and is now in the Place de la Concorde, Paris.

THINKER
This priest seems to have a worried expression. In fact the lines on his forehead, bags under his eyes, and furrows around his mouth are meant to indicate a life of serious contemplation. He is bald because most priests had to remove their hair.

Winged sky goddess

Son of Horus who looked after mummified body of priestess

GOLDEN COFFIN
This is the coffin of a priestess who served the god Amun and performed songs in his honour during temple rituals. She had three coffins, of which this one, of gilded wood, is the most impressive. Her face is portrayed as she would like to look for eternity.

Sacred rituals

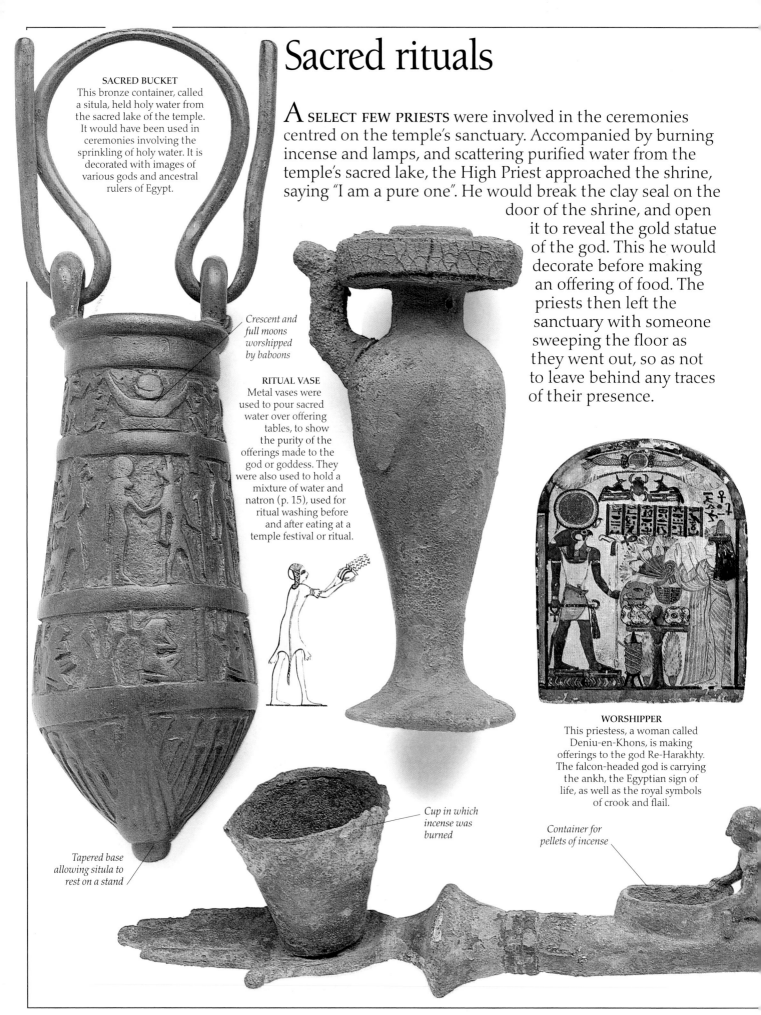

A SELECT FEW PRIESTS were involved in the ceremonies centred on the temple's sanctuary. Accompanied by burning incense and lamps, and scattering purified water from the temple's sacred lake, the High Priest approached the shrine, saying "I am a pure one". He would break the clay seal on the door of the shrine, and open it to reveal the gold statue of the god. This he would decorate before making an offering of food. The priests then left the sanctuary with someone sweeping the floor as they went out, so as not to leave behind any traces of their presence.

SACRED BUCKET
This bronze container, called a situla, held holy water from the sacred lake of the temple. It would have been used in ceremonies involving the sprinkling of holy water. It is decorated with images of various gods and ancestral rulers of Egypt.

Crescent and full moons worshipped by baboons

RITUAL VASE
Metal vases were used to pour sacred water over offering tables, to show the purity of the offerings made to the god or goddess. They were also used to hold a mixture of water and natron (p. 15), used for ritual washing before and after eating at a temple festival or ritual.

WORSHIPPER
This priestess, a woman called Deniu-en-Khons, is making offerings to the god Re-Harakhty. The falcon-headed god is carrying the ankh, the Egyptian sign of life, as well as the royal symbols of crook and flail.

Cup in which incense was burned

Container for pellets of incense

Tapered base allowing situla to rest on a stand

PRIESTLY PROCESSION
This group of priests are shaven headed - priests removed their hair to ensure cleanliness. Their leader is carrying an incense burner and scattering sacred water.

Baboon

Bird

Jackal

Frog

MAKING OFFERINGS
This bronze plaque shows a priest pouring sacred water over some offerings. Round loaves of bread and a vase of liquid are being offered to the god. At the front is a channel through which the holy water could drain away.

This is one of many temple paintings showing incense burners in use

AIR FRESHENER
Incense burns with an aroma that rises with the smoke. It was used in temples to attract the attention of the god with a pleasant fragrance, and to purify the atmosphere in the temple. This bronze incense burner has the head of the hawk god at one end.

STANDARD FINIAL
Priests carried standards in their processions through the temples. All that has survived of these are the emblems on top of the supporting poles. This one shows a bundle of papyrus plants and is topped by the falcon-god Horus, who is identified with the king of Egypt. Horus wears the combined crowns of Upper and Lower Egypt.

Goddess Mut

Head of Hathor

Khonsu

CULT MIRROR
Objects normally used for beautification, such as mirrors and cosmetic palettes, were placed in the temples for the use of the god. This example has a design that is full of religious symbols. From its handle, a crescent rises toward a hawk, suggesting a moon god such as Khonsu. Heads of the goddess Hathor adorn the columns on the face of the mirror itself. The goddess Mut (wife of the king of the gods and mother of Khonsu) is the figure being presented with a mirror in the centre.

Ivory handle

Scribes and scholars

Sᴄʀɪʙᴇꜱ ᴡᴇʀᴇ ɴᴇᴀʀ ᴛʜᴇ ᴛᴏᴘ of Egyptian society and capable scribes could do very well - one, Horemheb, even became king. The training was rigorous. From the age of nine you had to train for about five years. This was a problem because pupils could see children of their own age playing in the fields. Papyri have been discovered containing rebukes from senior to junior scribes about neglecting lessons; sometimes corporal punishment was recommended. One form of encouragement offered to pupils was a list of the defects of other professions - exaggerated, of course. For example, jewellers and metalworkers were said to choke on the heat of their furnaces, weavers had to put up with cramped conditions. But the scribe could look forward to authority, freedom from taxes and national service during times of flood, and immortality through his writings.

READY FOR WORK
This young scribe is shown sitting cross-legged with his papyrus scroll on his knees. Scribes are usually shown seated like this in Egyptian art.

Hole for ink

Bushy top of plant

GOOSE CENSUS
This scribe is counting geese on a nobleman's estate. He will enter the total on his scroll, for taxation records. His basket-work "briefcase" is in front of him, and his palettes and brushes are under his arm.

Stem used for writing material

Outer rind peeled away

Alternate layers

PAPYRUS
This triangular-stemmed reed about 4 m (12 ft) tall grew widely along the banks of the Nile, but vanished due to over-use for boats, baskets, sandals, rope, and writing material. Attempts are now being made to reintroduce it into Egypt.

Inner pith cut into strips

Stone

Mallet

MAKING A PAPYRUS SHEET
The strips of pith were arranged in two layers, one set horizontal, the next vertical, above each other. They were covered with linen and heavy pressure was applied with stones or a mallet. Eventually the strips would weld together in their own sap.

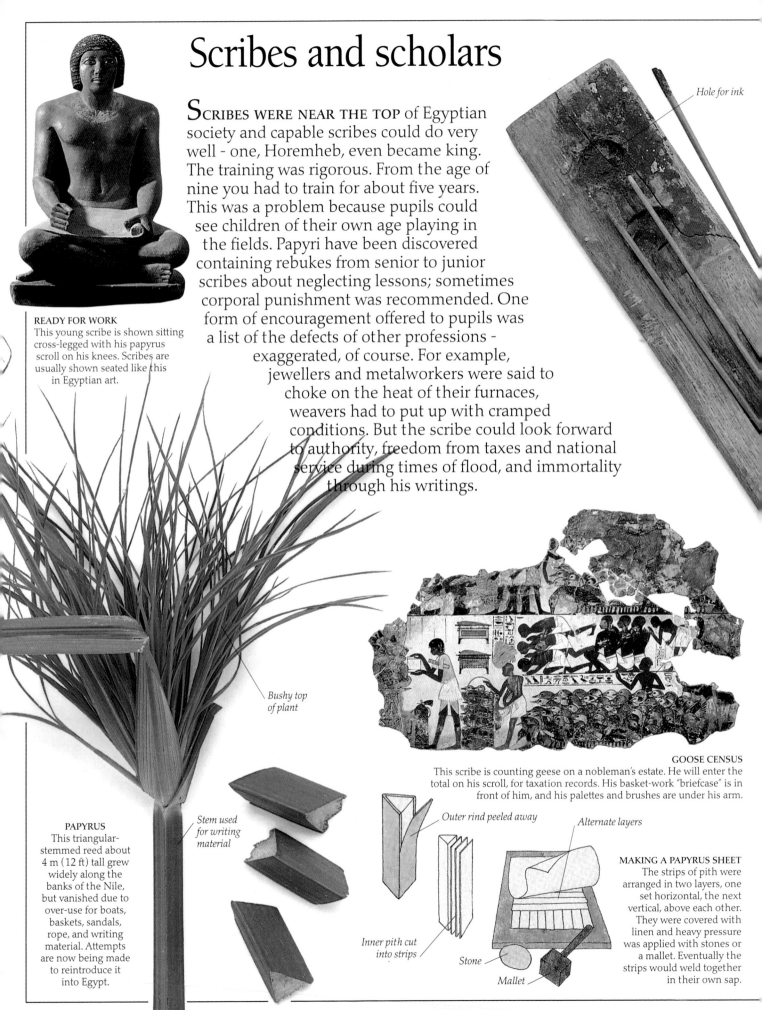

Grinder for crushing pigments

BASALT PALETTE
This palette is inscribed with a royal name, indicating that the scribe who used it was in the service of the palace. The pigments could be made from charcoal or soot to give black, or from red ochre, or blue or green minerals.

Draughtsmen

Egyptian artists were professional scribes who specialized in draughtsmanship for royal or funerary monuments. From unfinished tombs like that of King Horemheb it is possible to see all the stages involved in painting. First junior draughtsmen drew the scenes in red ochre on the dry plaster. Next senior artists might make corrections in black outline. The painters would then fill in the outlines with colour, or sculptors would cut away the background plaster to form a relief for painting.

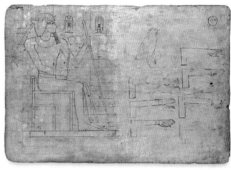

SKETCHPAD
A red ochre grid allowed the artist to divide the human body into squares to give the right proportions in this practice drawing of King Tuthmosis III.

WOODEN PALETTE
Most scribes had a wooden palette like this. It was portable, because the scribe might have to travel on business or to gather taxes.

Name of Ramesses I

SCRIBES AND SUPERVISOR
Busy writing on their scrolls, these two scribes appear to be writing down the words of the standing overseer. Notice the "briefcase" and document container in front of them.

Reed brushes for precision writing

SIGN FOR SCRIBE
This hieroglyphic sign shows a brush holder, a water pot for mixing pigments, and a palette, together making up the Egyptian word for a qualified scribe. The word was pronounced "sesh".

BRUSHES
The thick rope brush made of papyrus twine would have been used by painters covering large wall surfaces in tombs or temples. The other is also a painter's brush, perhaps used to paint thick hieroglyphs on huge statues.

Writing

SCRIBES HAD TO BE EXPERTS in writing hieroglyphs, an elaborate form of picture-writing with about 700 different signs. It was deliberately kept complicated so that not too many people could use it and the scribes kept their special position. Hieroglyphs were used on state monuments, temples, tombs, and religious papyri. They could be written from left to right, right to left, or top to bottom. For business contracts, letters, and stories, scribes used a different form of writing (script), called hieratic, which was a fast-written version of hieroglyphs, always running from right to left. Later on an even more rapid script evolved. Called demotic, it was often used for legal documents. Scribes living at the end of the Egyptian civilization also had to be able to write Greek, the language of their overlords.

IMHOTEP
This talented scribe lived 4,500 years ago. He was High Priest of the sun-god as well as being the designer of the first pyramid, at Saqqara. After his death he became accredited with limitless wisdom and was eventually turned into a god. Here he is unrolling a papyrus scroll.

LABEL
Scribes used tags like this to label their scrolls. This one tells us that its papyrus was written in the reign of Amenhotep III and told a story about a fig tree.

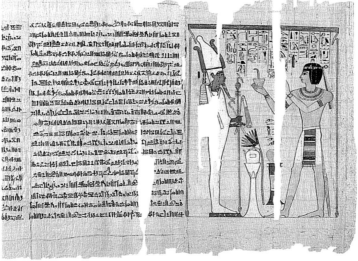

TWO SCRIPTS
On papyrus, scribes usually used the fast form of writing called hieratic. On this example, hieroglyphs appear above the picture of a high priest making an offering to the god Osiris. To the left is the script in hieratic.

ROYAL DOOR PLATE
The hieroglyphs on this metal plate read: "There shall always exist the Son of Re whom he loves, Amenhotep the god, ruler of Thebes".

King's name contained in oval border called a cartouche

CYLINDER SEAL
Seals like this were an early way of proving ownership or authority. This one bears the name of King Meryre, and also the name of one his officials who was obviously the owner of the seal. To the right is an impression showing the complete surface of the seal.

Cartouche bearing name of King Meryre

Name of Meryre's official

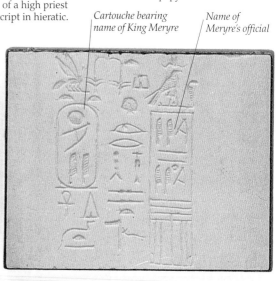

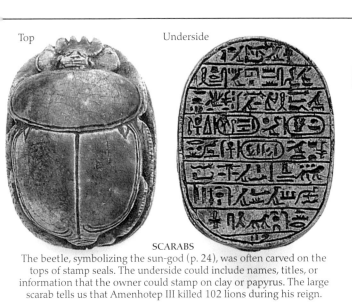

Top   Underside

Small scarab

SCARABS
The beetle, symbolizing the sun-god (p. 24), was often carved on the tops of stamp seals. The underside could include names, titles, or information that the owner could stamp on clay or papyrus. The large scarab tells us that Amenhotep III killed 102 lions during his reign.

The Rosetta Stone
When the last temple was closed in the 6th century CE, the skill of reading hieroglyphs was lost until the discovery of this stone in 1799. On the stone are three scripts. The bottom section is in Greek, the centre in demotic, and the top is in hieroglyphs. The stone was first set up in a temple. It was an elaborate "thank you" to the Greek ruler of Egypt Ptolemy V, who reigned in the 2nd century BCE, for benefits that he had given to the priests. The three scripts contained the same text, so allowing the hieroglyphs to be translated.

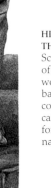

HIEROGLYPHS AND THEIR ORIGINS
Scribes chose pictures of their script from the world around them. The barn owl represented the consonant "m"; on the carving in the picture it forms part of the royal name "Amen em hat".

JEAN-FRANÇOIS CHAMPOLLION
French archaeologist, Jean-François Champollion spent many years deciphering the symbols on a slab of basalt found at Rosetta in the western Delta. His work on the Rosetta stone, as it is now called, was an important breakthrough in the translation of ancient hieroglyphics.

DECIPHERING THE STONE
When it was known that the stone contained royal names such as Ptolemy, their equivalents in hieroglyphs could be found at the top of the stone. From this information, the hieroglyphs making other words were worked out and the text was gradually deciphered.

NOTEBOOK
Some hieroglyphic signs needed a lot of practice from pupil scribes. Here a scribe has got carried away drawing the duckling hieroglyph, which was used in writing the word for "prime minister". The scribe has also practised drawing the head of a lion, which is used in one of the scenes in the Book of the Dead.

Weapons of war

Soldiers carrying spears, shields, and battle-axes, being given orders by trumpet. Chariots were not introduced until c. 1600 BCE.

SOLDIERS FIRST PLAYED an important role in Egypt in around 3000 BCE. Later on, the pharaohs undertook military campaigns abroad in Palestine, Syria, and Nubia. The Egyptian army was well organized. It had a hierarchy of officers, from the pharaoh himself down to officers in charge of groups of 50 soldiers, and army scribes who wrote dispatches and records of the campaigns. There were both infantry and chariot troops. Egyptian chariots, each manned by two soldiers and pulled by two horses, were made of wood. They acted as mobile firing platforms from which archers could attack the enemy. In peacetime, soldiers would take part in civil tasks such as digging irrigation canals or transporting stone from the desert for the king's tomb.

Ceremonial axe with openwork head

Battle axe

Long blade for "slicing" action

Silver-shafted axe

KING AT WAR
This scene from the side of a box discovered in Tutankhamun's tomb shows the king attacking enemies from Nubia. He rides alone in a chariot drawn by two horses, followed by fanbearers. In real life he would have had a charioteer to drive for him. His foes are falling in disarray.

ANCIENT AXES
The axe was used as a weapon all over the Middle East. The silver-handled axe has a long blade designed for a slicing movement. The openwork axe is ceremonial, but could also have made an effective weapon, like the plainer axe to the right.

Silver nail

FINGER GUARD
Archers would sometimes draw their bow strings into a triangular shape, pulling them back almost to their ears. This bone guard protected the archer's finger from pain caused by the taut animal gut of the string as he drew his bow.

Flint heads

SMALL BUT DEADLY
The first arrowheads were made of flint or a hard wood like ebony. Later bronze was used. The horseshoe shapes were designed to wound, while the sharp triangular arrowheads were meant to kill the victim outright.

Bronze heads

TRUSTY BLADES
With straighter handles than daggers, swords were influenced by a middle-eastern design. They had the advantage that they could be gripped tightly; they could also have a longer blade, attached with rivets.

ON THE MARCH
Protected by large shields made of wood rather than heavy armour, these infantry soldiers are armed with battle axes and spears.

ARROW
With its blunt tip and reed shaft, this may have been a hunter's weapon, although in its size it resembles a soldier's arrow.

Dagger

Tutankhamun wears a wrist protector

MEDALS
Gold flies were given to a soldier who had done well in combat, persistently "stinging" the enemy.

DEADLY DAGGER
Traditional Egyptian daggers have fine tapered copper blades decorated with stripes. The wide top of the blade is rivetted to the handle. The pommel of ivory or bone on top of the handle fitted into the palm of the hand. Daggers could be carried openly in the belt of a kilt or - in wooden sheaths overlaid with gold.

Short sword

Long sword

WRIST PROTECTOR
An archer wore this guard on his left wrist to protect himself from the whip of the bowstring when firing an arrow. The tongue-shaped section reached towards the palm.

Sailing on the Nile

THE NILE was the main highway of Egypt. The earliest boats were made of papyrus but dockyards along the Nile were soon busy making boats out of timber. Our best evidence for the skill of the shipbuilders is a boat over 40 m (130 ft) long built for King Khufu around 4,500 years ago and discovered in a pit next to the Great Pyramid (pp. 20–21). It was a keel-less ceremonial barge with a cabin for the king and was probably intended for Khufu's journey with the sun-god in the afterlife. Temple reliefs show other large boats transporting huge columns and obelisks of granite from the quarries of Aswan to sites hundreds of miles away. From small cargo boats for carrying grain to state ships for kings and high officials we get a full picture of transport on the Nile. The Egyptians gave ships names like we do today. For example, one commander started off in a ship called "Northern" and got promoted to the ship "Rising in Memphis".

THE RA EXPEDITION
The first Egyptian boats were made of papyrus reed stalks bunched together (and in plentiful supply along the Nile). For ocean voyages Egyptians used large boats made of wood. Explorer Thor Heyerdhal sailed his papyrus boat "Ra" from Egypt to America, showing such a vessel might have survived an ocean crossing.

GONE FISHING
These skiffs are made of bundles of papyrus reeds tied together with twine. They are each propelled by two oarsmen and are linked to each other by the dragnet. You can see some of the fish trapped in it as well as the floats around the edges of the net. The fishermen are about to pull the net in with the catch.

Ox-hide canopy

Steering oar

Steersman

Owner of the boat

DHOW
In the 19th century dhows were as common on the Nile as their ancient ancestors.

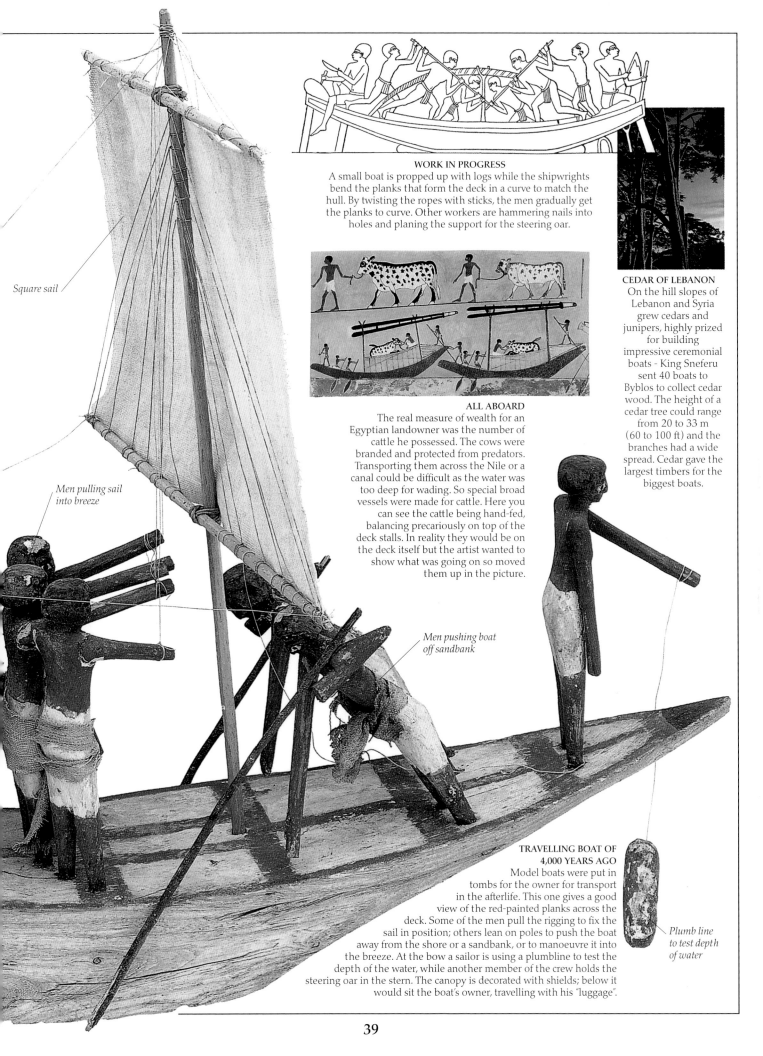

WORK IN PROGRESS
A small boat is propped up with logs while the shipwrights bend the planks that form the deck in a curve to match the hull. By twisting the ropes with sticks, the men gradually get the planks to curve. Other workers are hammering nails into holes and planing the support for the steering oar.

CEDAR OF LEBANON
On the hill slopes of Lebanon and Syria grew cedars and junipers, highly prized for building impressive ceremonial boats - King Sneferu sent 40 boats to Byblos to collect cedar wood. The height of a cedar tree could range from 20 to 33 m (60 to 100 ft) and the branches had a wide spread. Cedar gave the largest timbers for the biggest boats.

Square sail

Men pulling sail into breeze

Men pushing boat off sandbank

ALL ABOARD
The real measure of wealth for an Egyptian landowner was the number of cattle he possessed. The cows were branded and protected from predators. Transporting them across the Nile or a canal could be difficult as the water was too deep for wading. So special broad vessels were made for cattle. Here you can see the cattle being hand-fed, balancing precariously on top of the deck stalls. In reality they would be on the deck itself but the artist wanted to show what was going on so moved them up in the picture.

TRAVELLING BOAT OF 4,000 YEARS AGO
Model boats were put in tombs for the owner for transport in the afterlife. This one gives a good view of the red-painted planks across the deck. Some of the men pull the rigging to fix the sail in position; others lean on poles to push the boat away from the shore or a sandbank, or to manoeuvre it into the breeze. At the bow a sailor is using a plumbline to test the depth of the water, while another member of the crew holds the steering oar in the stern. The canopy is decorated with shields; below it would sit the boat's owner, travelling with his "luggage".

Plumb line to test depth of water

Buying and selling

E GYPT WAS THE WEALTHIEST COUNTRY of the ancient world. Some of the gold from the mines of the eastern desert and Nubia was sent abroad in the form of gifts to foreign rulers like the king of Babylon. Princesses and manufactured goods were sent in exchange to the pharaoh. Although the pharaohs at times controlled long stretches of the Nile beyond the southern frontier at Aswan, the produce of deep equatorial Africa was obtained through trade with the princes of Nubia, the area south of the first cataract of the Nile. An important exchange post was at Kerma, near the third cataract of the Nile. Egyptian merchants brought back a variety of goods like panther skins, greyhounds, giraffe tails for fly whisks, elephant tusks, and animals such as baboons and lions for the temples or palace.

BARTERING
This was a common way of buying goods. You might exchange a pair of sandals for a fine walking stick or a linen garment for a large quantity of food. These men are carrying saleable items such as ducks and a jar of wine in a rope basket.

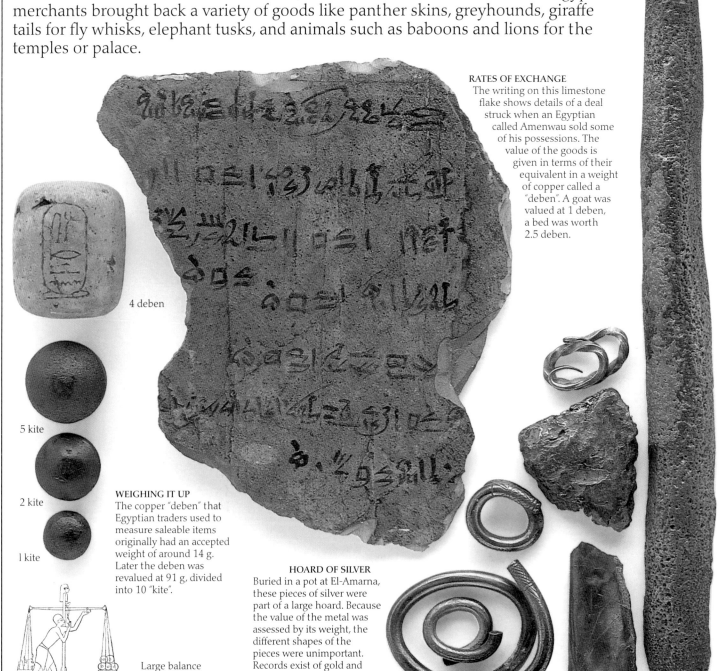

RATES OF EXCHANGE
The writing on this limestone flake shows details of a deal struck when an Egyptian called Amenwau sold some of his possessions. The value of the goods is given in terms of their equivalent in a weight of copper called a "deben". A goat was valued at 1 deben, a bed was worth 2.5 deben.

4 deben

5 kite

2 kite

1 kite

WEIGHING IT UP
The copper "deben" that Egyptian traders used to measure saleable items originally had an accepted weight of around 14 g. Later the deben was revalued at 91 g, divided into 10 "kite".

Large balance for weighing produce

HOARD OF SILVER
Buried in a pot at El-Amarna, these pieces of silver were part of a large hoard. Because the value of the metal was assessed by its weight, the different shapes of the pieces were unimportant. Records exist of gold and copper being weighed out and used as payments in a similar way.

Unloading pottery wine jars from a Nile boat belonging to a high official

IVORY DISH
Elephant tusks came to Egypt via the trade with Nubia and were carved into luxury items like this cosmetic spoon. If the supply of ivory from Nubia fell short, the teeth of hippos could be used instead. The design of this cosmetic spoon includes the head of Hathor, goddess of beauty and foreign countries.

CASSIA
The dried bark of a type of laurel tree, cassia was brought from India. The Egyptians used it for perfume and incense.

Ivory fittings

Ebony handle

Hathor has the ears of the cow, her sacred animal

The land of Punt

The Egyptians thought of the land of Punt as a remote and exotic place. We do not know exactly where it was, but the most frequent route to it seems to have been along the coast of the Red Sea and then inland towards the river Atbara, a tributary of the Nile. In the 15th century BCE, Queen Hatshepsut sent five boats to Punt. Eventually the boats pulled in at a port on the coast of eastern Sudan. From here the queen's representatives were taken some way inland. Here they saw people who lived in houses on stilts to protect them from wild animals. Incense was the main cargo they brought back.

FRANKINCENSE
In eastern Sudan, Ethiopia, Somalia, and Yemen grew trees that yielded this fragrant gum resin.

GIFTS FROM SYRIA
These Syrian princes are bringing tribute to the pharaoh. They offer gold vases decorated with lotus flowers, and perfume containers in gold, lapis lazuli, or ivory. One Syrian prince brings his daughter to be brought up at court.

FLY WHISK
Ebony, used in this fly whisk, was a highly valued import from central Africa. It was bought in shipments of logs from the Nubians. Courtiers used to carry fly whisks, and these became signs of their status.

Lapis lazuli bull set in gold

LAPIS LAZULI
Merchants from Afghanistan brought this valuable stone to trading centres like Byblos in Lebanon. The Egyptians prized this gem, and thought that the hair of the sun-god was made of lapis lazuli.

Unworked lapis lazuli

THE INCENSE TRADE
The myrrh and frankincense that the Egyptians carried back from Punt could have been brought from still further south. They took not only the gum resin but also whole trees to plant in front of Queen Hatshepsut's temple.

An Egyptian carpenter

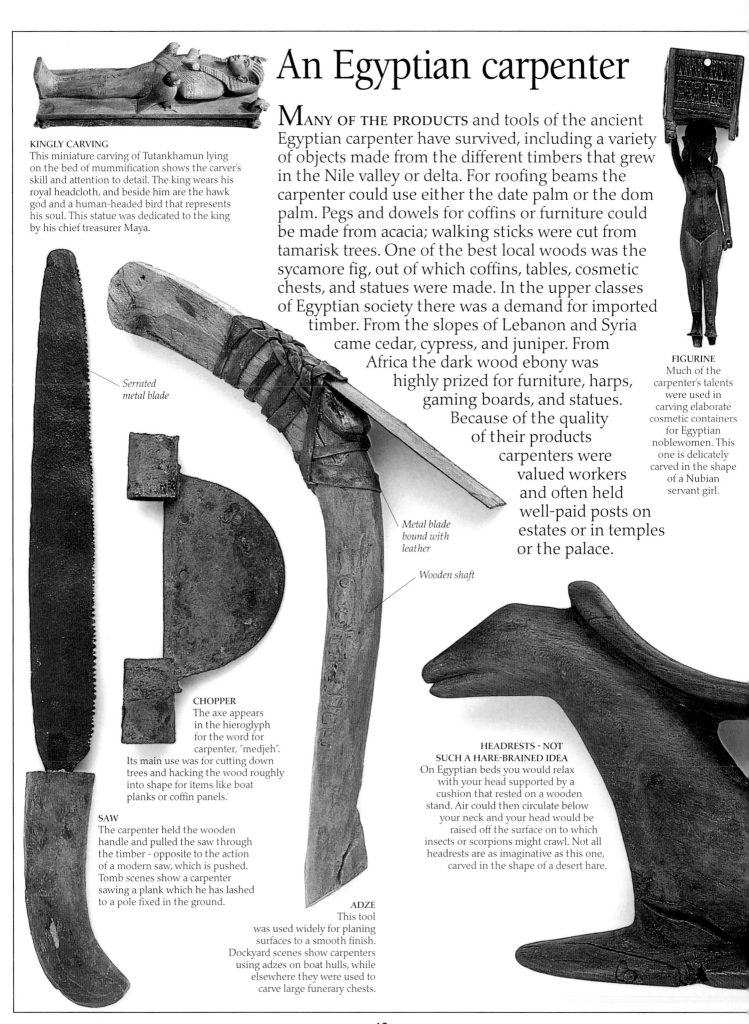

KINGLY CARVING
This miniature carving of Tutankhamun lying on the bed of mummification shows the carver's skill and attention to detail. The king wears his royal headcloth, and beside him are the hawk god and a human-headed bird that represents his soul. This statue was dedicated to the king by his chief treasurer Maya.

MANY OF THE PRODUCTS and tools of the ancient Egyptian carpenter have survived, including a variety of objects made from the different timbers that grew in the Nile valley or delta. For roofing beams the carpenter could use either the date palm or the dom palm. Pegs and dowels for coffins or furniture could be made from acacia; walking sticks were cut from tamarisk trees. One of the best local woods was the sycamore fig, out of which coffins, tables, cosmetic chests, and statues were made. In the upper classes of Egyptian society there was a demand for imported timber. From the slopes of Lebanon and Syria came cedar, cypress, and juniper. From Africa the dark wood ebony was highly prized for furniture, harps, gaming boards, and statues. Because of the quality of their products carpenters were valued workers and often held well-paid posts on estates or in temples or the palace.

FIGURINE
Much of the carpenter's talents were used in carving elaborate cosmetic containers for Egyptian noblewomen. This one is delicately carved in the shape of a Nubian servant girl.

Serrated metal blade

Metal blade bound with leather

Wooden shaft

CHOPPER
The axe appears in the hieroglyph for the word for carpenter, "medjeh". Its main use was for cutting down trees and hacking the wood roughly into shape for items like boat planks or coffin panels.

SAW
The carpenter held the wooden handle and pulled the saw through the timber - opposite to the action of a modern saw, which is pushed. Tomb scenes show a carpenter sawing a plank which he has lashed to a pole fixed in the ground.

HEADRESTS - NOT SUCH A HARE-BRAINED IDEA
On Egyptian beds you would relax with your head supported by a cushion that rested on a wooden stand. Air could then circulate below your neck and your head would be raised off the surface on to which insects or scorpions might crawl. Not all headrests are as imaginative as this one, carved in the shape of a desert hare.

ADZE
This tool was used widely for planing surfaces to a smooth finish. Dockyard scenes show carpenters using adzes on boat hulls, while elsewhere they were used to carve large funerary chests.

GOAT'S HEAD
Chairs, boxes, and chests were often decorated with animal features. A chair could have legs shaped like lion's paws; a throne could have arms surmounted by winged snakes or vultures. This small fragment has been exquisitely carved to show the horn, curly fleece, and beard of a goat. It probably came from the decoration of a chest.

MEN AT WORK
These two carpenters are putting the finishing touches to a large wooden casket that has been inlaid with colourful materials. One uses a mallet to hammer out a hole for a peg while the other is polishing the lid.

Hare's ears support pillow and head

BORING JOB
To bore a hole in a plank of wood the carpenter used a drill consisting of a metal or flint point in a shaft of wood. He placed it over the spot in the plank where he wanted the hole and rotated the cutting point using a bow. Sometimes a workmate would hold a heavy pebble over the shaft of the drill to create more pressure.

BRADAWL
"Starter holes" could be made with a bradawl, so that the bowdrill could get a grip. Bradawls were also used by shipwrights to mark the points on planks where wooden pegs were to be fitted.

CHISEL
A carpenter would need a chisel like this for intricate carving and for cutting hieroglyphs into the surfaces of large rectangular wooden coffins.

Twine

Wooden bow

Metal drill bit

SMOOTHING STONE
The rough surfaces left after carving could be smoothed down using a pebble. The highly polished finish of furniture was often achieved in this way.

DRILL
Carpenters often used a bow drill to make holes for pegs to join pieces of timber together. The wooden shaft of this bow-drill is well worn - it was obviously much used by its original owner.

43

Hunting, fishing, and fowling

At the time of the pharaohs farming produced an abundance of food, so hunting was mainly a recreation for kings and courtiers. In the Egyptian deserts they would be able to hunt wild bulls, gazelles, oryx, antelopes, and lions. King Amenhotep III was proud of killing over 100 fierce lions in ten years; he also killed over 90 wild bulls on one hunting expedition. Often there was no danger to the monarch at all if he went hunting - the bulls would be herded into an enclosure in the marshes and picked off one by one by the pharaoh in his chariot. To begin with, the courtiers hunted on foot, their followers fencing off areas to hem the animals in; later they too used chariots. As well as animals, the river was plentiful in fish, which could be caught with hooks or nets. The papyrus thickets also offered a variety of birds and geese. Here the technique was to hurl a throwstick as the wildfowl flew up from the thickets.

FAMILY OUTING
This nobleman is hunting birds in the papyrus marshes. He is using a snake-shaped throwstick, and the three herons he holds disguise his approach. He has brought his cat, which has caught three birds. With him are his daughter, sitting in the boat, and his elegant wife - who is hardly dressed for the hunt!

Flat tips to weaken animal by piercing hide

Sharp tip to kill outright

Cleft end for bow string

ARROWS
Bows and arrows figure in some of the earliest monuments from ancient Egypt. Made of reeds, the arrows were tipped with ivory, bone, flint, obsidian, or metal.

THROW STICK
Shaped like boomerangs and made of wood, throwsticks were hurled at wildfowl in the hope of breaking the birds' necks or wings, or at least stunning them.

HUNTING THE HIPPO
This animal could cause havoc among reed boats on the Nile and to crops on land. So teams of men in papyrus boats would hunt the hippo, gradually weakening it by repeated spearing until it collapsed. They also used lassoes to hamper the creature's movements.

SPOILS OF THE DESERT
Desert hares are often shown in Egyptian hunting scenes. Sometimes a hare pierced with an arrow will still be trying to scramble to safety. Antelopes and gazelles were also found in the desert, and ostrich eggs were a desert delicacy.

HOOKS
Copper or bronze hooks were used for fishing by line. Once the fish were hooked out of the water they were gutted and dried in the sun.

WEIGHING THEM DOWN
Like fishermen today, the Egyptians used lead weights to keep their fishing nets under the water.

FISHING NET
This net was used by an Egyptian fisherman about 3,000 years ago. Nets like this made from reed and papyrus twine were made for trapping both birds and fish. They were kept in position by reed-floats and hauled in by the fisherman.

Courtiers used this type of harpoon to test their skill

Prong to attach rope

HARPOONS
Attached to reed or wooden shafts, metal harpoons were used to catch large game and fish. Symbolically a harpoon was held by kings in the ritual of spearing the hippopotamus of the god Seth. In reality one harpoon would not kill such a large creature and a series of harpoons would be required.

The Egyptians at home

HOUSES IN ANCIENT EGYPT were built from bricks made from the Nile mud. The mud was collected in leather buckets and taken to the building site. Here workers would add straw and pebbles to the mud to strengthen it and pour the mixture into wooden frames to make bricks. They would leave these out in the sun to dry. When a house was built, its walls would be covered with plaster, and the inside was often painted - either with patterns or scenes from nature. Inside, the houses were cool, as the small windows let in only a little light. Wealthy families had large houses. Beyond the hall would be bedrooms and private apartments, and stairs to the roof. The kitchen was some distance from the living rooms, to keep smells away. The Egyptians held parties in their homes, which the children enjoyed as much as their parents.

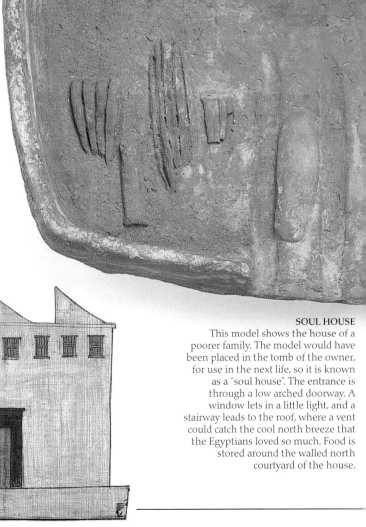

AROUND THE POOL
A pool was often the central feature of a wealthy family's garden. It would be stocked with lotuses and fish, and the water would be renewed regularly to keep it fresh. Poolside borders would be planted with shrubs and trees such as sycamore figs, date palms, and acacia trees.

HOME COMFORTS
This is a typical home belonging to a successful official, the royal scribe Nakht. Made of mud bricks, the walls were coated with limestone plaster. Grille windows high on the walls let in only a little sunlight and dust, while vents trap the cool north wind. In front would be a garden with a pool and trees, in which Nakht and his wife could relax.

SOUL HOUSE
This model shows the house of a poorer family. The model would have been placed in the tomb of the owner, for use in the next life, so it is known as a "soul house". The entrance is through a low arched doorway. A window lets in a little light, and a stairway leads to the roof, where a vent could catch the cool north breeze that the Egyptians loved so much. Food is stored around the walled north courtyard of the house.

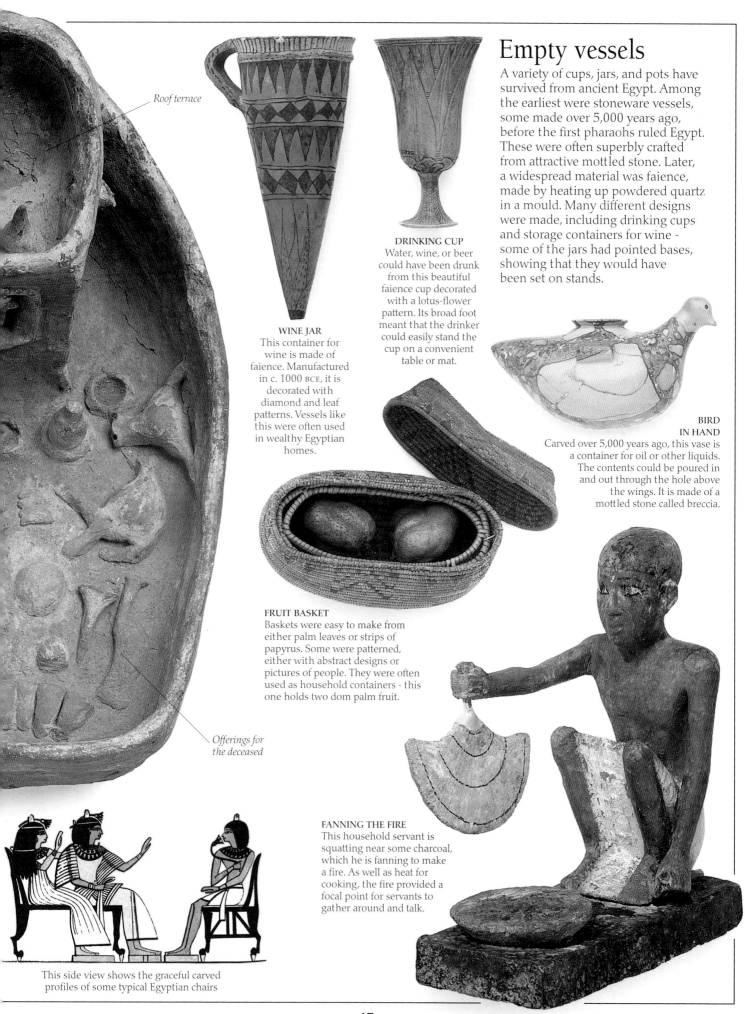

Roof terrace

Offerings for the deceased

Empty vessels

A variety of cups, jars, and pots have survived from ancient Egypt. Among the earliest were stoneware vessels, some made over 5,000 years ago, before the first pharaohs ruled Egypt. These were often superbly crafted from attractive mottled stone. Later, a widespread material was faience, made by heating up powdered quartz in a mould. Many different designs were made, including drinking cups and storage containers for wine - some of the jars had pointed bases, showing that they would have been set on stands.

WINE JAR
This container for wine is made of faience. Manufactured in c. 1000 BCE, it is decorated with diamond and leaf patterns. Vessels like this were often used in wealthy Egyptian homes.

DRINKING CUP
Water, wine, or beer could have been drunk from this beautiful faience cup decorated with a lotus-flower pattern. Its broad foot meant that the drinker could easily stand the cup on a convenient table or mat.

BIRD IN HAND
Carved over 5,000 years ago, this vase is a container for oil or other liquids. The contents could be poured in and out through the hole above the wings. It is made of a mottled stone called breccia.

FRUIT BASKET
Baskets were easy to make from either palm leaves or strips of papyrus. Some were patterned, either with abstract designs or pictures of people. They were often used as household containers - this one holds two dom palm fruit.

FANNING THE FIRE
This household servant is squatting near some charcoal, which he is fanning to make a fire. As well as heat for cooking, the fire provided a focal point for servants to gather around and talk.

This side view shows the graceful carved profiles of some typical Egyptian chairs

Food and drink

THE FERTILE MUD deposited by the annual Nile flood allowed farmers to grow barley and emmer wheat, the mainstay of the Egyptian diet. Stored in granaries, these crops were turned into bread or beer. The flood plain also lent itself to the cultivation of vegetables such as onions, garlic, leeks, beans, lentils, and lettuce. There were also gourds, dates and figs, cucumbers and melons, but no citrus fruits. Egyptian bakers made cakes of many shapes and sizes, sweetened by dates or by honey gathered from conical pottery beehives. Grapes grown in the Nile delta or oases of the western desert were plucked for wine-making or drying into raisins. The less well-off people would have less meat and poultry, and more fish. The spread at banquets was extremely varied - from ducks, geese, and oxen to oryx and gazelle. There were also pigs sheep, and goats, which could be boiled or roasted.

BUTCHERS AT WORK
An ox was slaughtered by tying three of its feet together, pushing it on its side, and cutting its throat. The free leg was cut, and sometimes given as a religious offering.

IN THE VINEYARD
Two men pluck bunches of grapes from the vines. This job was often given to foreign settlers or prisoners from the Middle East or Nubia. The grapes would then be taken to be crushed by treading.

BREAD
More than 3,000 years old, this bread was baked from barley dough. Its texture is tough: flour often contained grit that got in during grinding. Studies of mummies have shown how coarse bread made Egyptians' teeth wear away.

STRAINER
This wooden syphon with its perforated mouthpiece was used for making beer more palatable. Made from mashed loaves of barley-bread, Egyptian beer was very thick and needed to be strained either through a basket or with a syphon.

Perforations for straining

A Syrian soldier serving the pharaoh Akhenaten is sitting drinking beer through a syphon

GRAPES
The Egyptians grew most of their grapes in the north, just as they do today. Both red and green grapes provided the fermented juice for wine. They also imported wine from Syria and Greece.

DELICIOUS DATES
Dates were eaten fresh at harvest time in August or could be dried or conserved in a sweet mash. A date wine was made and the sap could also be made into wine.

BABOON WHO DOES NOT GIVE A FIG!
The fruit of the sycamore fig was held in high esteem in ancient Egypt. The modern examples are easily identifiable as the same as those on this sketch. Baboons loved figs and are often shown helping themselves from bowls or straight from the trees.

Modern fig

PALM-TREE FRUIT
These dom-palm fruit come from a 3,000-year-old tomb offering. The fruit have a gingery taste. The outer case of the nut is so tough it could be used as the top end of a drill.

Large pomegranate produced by modern agriculture

EGYPTIAN BANQUET
Scribes and nobles were able to enjoy a wide variety of meat, poultry, and fruit. This rich and colourful display of food and drink is from a party scene at a Theban banquet. Wine jars are fixed with their pointed bases in racks and garlanded with leaves. The courses included cakes, baskets of figs and bunches of grapes, the head of a calf, the heart and foreleg of an ox, a plucked goose, and a twist of onions.

POMEGRANATES
The pomegranate was introduced to Egypt from the Middle East and its fruit were soon popular. This dish contains pomegranates that were originally part of a tomb offering. The shape of the fruit was used as a model for jewellery and drinking cups. The skin may have been used to produce a yellowish dye.

Ancient fruit

Song and dance

THE EGYPTIANS ENJOYED LIFE to the full. Party scenes on tomb walls, songs on papyri, and musical instruments show us how much music and revelry meant to them. They had great public festivals, at which thousands of people were entertained with singing and music from flutes, harps, and castanets, and much wine was drunk. Music was also performed on more everyday occasions. Vintagers pressed grapes for wine while men clapped rhythm sticks together; farmworkers sang to their oxen as they threshed the corn with their hooves; a princess would play the harp while her husband relaxed on a divan; dancers would turn somersaults alongside processions. We do not know exactly what Egyptian music sounded like, but a small orchestra at a banquet could have string, wind, and percussions sections, and the music probably had a strong beat.

Twine holds discs together

Double crown of Upper and Lower Egypt

Dancing girls shake their bodies to the rhythm of the music

SONG AND DANCE
This section from a tomb painting shows a group of dancers and an orchestra of women playing a song in praise of nature. The frontal view shown in this picture is very unusual in Egyptian art.

FIVE-STRINGED HARP
Harps varied greatly in size - some were as tall as the player. The number of strings also varied, from four to over twenty. The king's head may indicate that the harp belonged to a court musician.

Head of king wearing striped headcloth

Wooden body

Lotus-blossom design

CRASH!
Bronze cymbals could emphasize the rhythm of a piece of music in a series of sharp metallic clashes. Combined with drums and tambourines the cymbals gave music a rousing quality.

Hawk's head terminal

Priestess carrying a sistrum

Discs rattled when shaken

Tuning peg

Animal gut strings

FLUTE
The pipe or flute is one of the most ancient instruments. They were usually made of reeds or wood. This wooden pipe would be blown directly through its reinforced mouthpiece.

Head of Hathor

Wedjat eye tattoo

SACRED RATTLE
The sistrum was carried by noblewomen and priestesses at ceremonies. They used it together with a sacred necklace known as a "menat". It was linked with the cult of the goddess Hathor, who stood for joy and fondness for music and dance.

BONE CLAPPERS
These clappers were probably joined by papyrus twine. They could then be held in one hand and played in the same way that a modern Spanish dancer would use castanets.

PLAYING THE HARP
This wooden model represents a girl playing a harp which she holds against her body. In real life she would rest the harp on a stand while she plucked the strings. Her role was to provide music at parties in the afterlife.

Lyre and double-flute players from a painting at Thebes

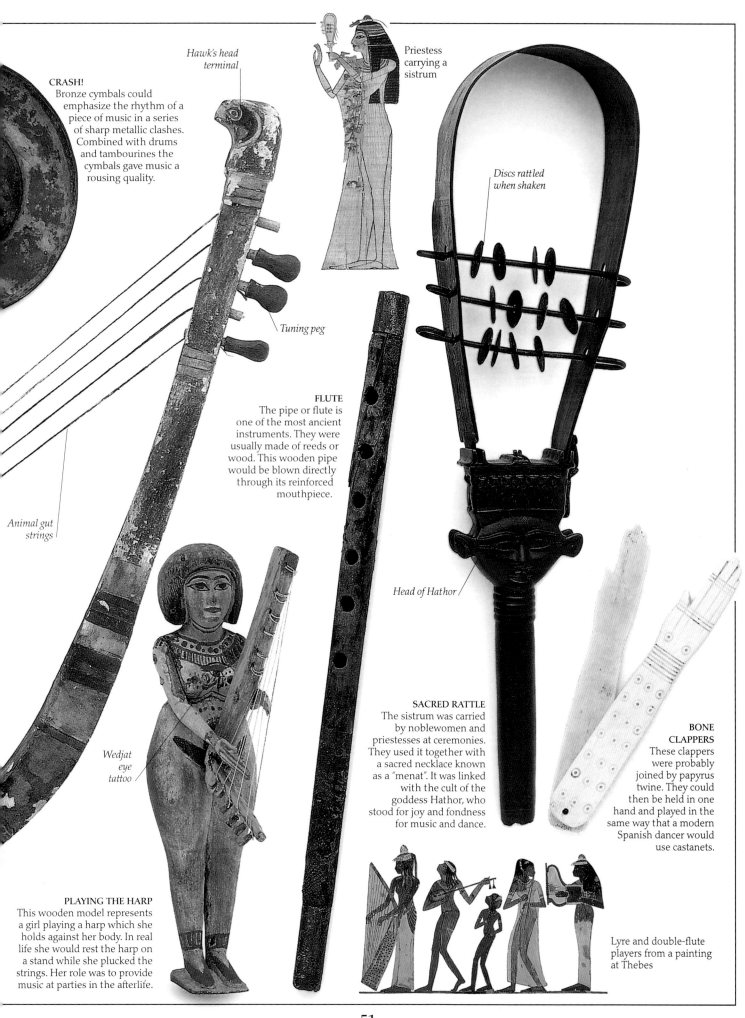

51

Toys and games

GAME PIECE
This carved lion head could have been used as a counter in a number of games.

EVEN AS CHILDREN, the ancient Egyptians enjoyed life. Some of the games they played are still loved by children today, such as "khuzza lawizza", or leapfrog, and tug-of-war. There are also Egyptian paintings showing boys playing soldiers and girls holding hands in a sort of spinning dance. Then there were board games, like snake and the more complicated senet, and a number of toys from model animals and dolls to balls. The Egyptians were also great storytellers, and kept their children amused with popular tales of imagination and enchantment. In one example, a magical wax toy crocodile turns into a real one when thrown into the water - a relevant story for people who lived under the threat of being eaten by crocodiles every day of their lives.

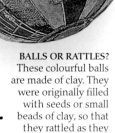

BALLS OR RATTLES?
These colourful balls are made of clay. They were originally filled with seeds or small beads of clay, so that they rattled as they were thrown.

DOLL OR GIRLFRIEND?
The Egyptians made dolls out of wood, with hair of clay beads attached to lengths of twine. Dolls like this one may have been for children, or they may have been made to put in someone's tomb, to act as a companion in the afterlife.

BALL GAMES
A popular pastime, especially for girls, was throwing and catching balls. This was not just done standing, but also on piggy-back or leaping high into the air.

HORSE ON WHEELS
The Egyptians used horses to pull chariots and also on hunting trips. Horse-riding became a favourite pastime of the pharaohs. This toy horse, dating from Roman Egypt, has a saddle mat thrown over it. It was pulled along by a rope through the muzzle.

Twine to move lower jaw

TOY MOUSE
This wooden mouse had a twine fitted to it, which a child could pull to make the tail go up and down.

ROAR OR MIAOW?
This toy does not seem to know whether it is a cat or a lion. Roughly carved from wood into a cat-like shape, its main attraction is its movable lower jaw, attached to some twine.

The game of senet

This board game symbolized a struggle against the forces of evil that tried to prevent you from reaching the kingdom of the god Osiris. On the thirty squares of the board were images that could stand for advantages like "beauty" or "power", or for perils, like the spearing of a hippo. There were two sets of counters and moves were made according to the way throwsticks landed.

YOUR MOVE
This papyrus from the Book of the Dead of the scribe Ani shows Ani and his wife Tutu playing senet. In spite of the fact that the artist has drawn Tutu sitting behind her husband in a rather formal pose, both seem to be enjoying their game.

SPINNING TOPS
A vigorous twist of the fingers or a tug on some papyrus twine wound on to the cone would set these tops spinning. They were made of powdered quartz formed in a mould and then glazed. Toys of cheap materials like this meant that even the poorest families could give their children a few amusing games.

FIT FOR A KING
Tutankhamun was buried with four senet boards of which this ebony and ivory board is the finest. It is fitted with a drawer for the counters and fixed on legs that have been delicately carved in the shape of animals' feet.

Hieroglyph of pharaoh's name

Stone ball used in the snake game

THE GAME OF SNAKE
One of the earliest board games discovered in Egypt was called "snake" because the stone board represented a serpent coiled with its head in the centre. The winner would be the first to move his or her counter around the squares on the snake's body to the middle. The stone balls are sometimes carved with the names of some of Egypt's earliest pharaohs.

From fabric to finery

FROM THE EARLIEST TIMES, flax provided linen for clothes for everyone in ancient Egypt. The earliest picture of a loom in Egypt is on a pottery bowl dated to c. 3000 BCE and flax was used for thousands of years after this. A pharaoh would have exceptionally fine linen; workers wore loincloths of coarser fabric. They had clever ways of avoiding wear on linen clothes - soldiers would cover the rear of their kilts with leather netting; domestic servants wore nets of cheap but colourful beads over their dresses. The basic courtier's kilt consisted of a linen cloth wrapped around the waist and secured by a knot - often elaborately tied. Gradually cloaks developed for use as overgarments. Women wore long, sheath-like dresses often with beautifully pleated cloaks. There are still only vague ideas about how the Egyptians got pleats into their clothes - perhaps it involved a board with a grooved surface. Probably the number of pleats is exaggerated in many statues. The Egyptians learned the art of dying their clothes in coloured patterns from the Middle East, but the technique was never widespread.

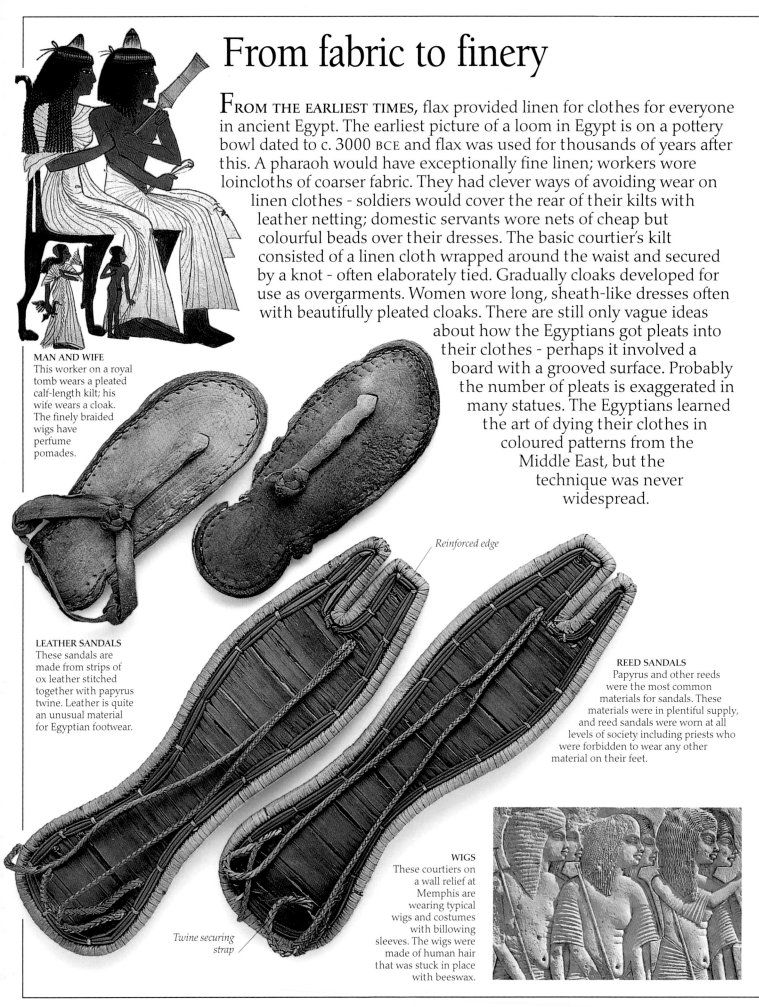

MAN AND WIFE
This worker on a royal tomb wears a pleated calf-length kilt; his wife wears a cloak. The finely braided wigs have perfume pomades.

LEATHER SANDALS
These sandals are made from strips of ox leather stitched together with papyrus twine. Leather is quite an unusual material for Egyptian footwear.

Reinforced edge

REED SANDALS
Papyrus and other reeds were the most common materials for sandals. These materials were in plentiful supply, and reed sandals were worn at all levels of society including priests who were forbidden to wear any other material on their feet.

Twine securing strap

WIGS
These courtiers on a wall relief at Memphis are wearing typical wigs and costumes with billowing sleeves. The wigs were made of human hair that was stuck in place with beeswax.

PRINCESS OR QUEEN?
This statue is one of many intriguing works of art that survives from the reign of Akhenaten (p. 10). It represents Akhenaten's queen, Nefertiti, or one of her daughters. She is shown wearing a very fine garment of royal linen. The number of pleats may have been an artistic exaggeration, but the dress certainly would have many of them.

IN THE GROOVE
This grooved board may have been used for pleating. The damp garment would be pressed into the grooves.

FLAX COMB
The first stage in making linen was to remove the flax heads with a long comb like this one. Then the flax stems were soaked and beaten to separate the fibres from the stalk for combing again to prepare them for spinning.

LINEN SHEET
Types of linen in ancient Egypt ranged from coarse material like this, which most people would have used, to the finest gauze worn by kings and queens.

SPINDLE
The flax fibres were spun on sticks, or spindles, which had a weighted circular whorl on one end. Whorls dating from early dynastic times have been discovered.

SPINNER
This girl is using her left hand to draw the twisted slivers of fibres (the rove), which are attached to the rotating spindle balanced by the weight of the whorl.

55

All that glitters

YOU CAN SEE the glint of gold everywhere in Egyptian jewellery - mines between the Nile and the Red Sea coast yielded large quantities of this precious metal. The gold could be beaten into shape or cast in moulds. Goldsmiths also made patterns using a method called granulation, in which tiny granules of gold were attached to an object by soldering. Egyptian jewellers had access to many semi-precious stones from the deserts - the orange-red carnelian, the green feldspar, and the mauve amethyst. They also imported stones. From mines in the Sinai peninsula came the light blue turquoise and trade routes from Afghanistan brought rich blue lapis lazuli to Egypt. But Egyptian jewellers had no knowledge of stones like diamonds, emeralds, or rubies.

Rings of gold being brought to Egypt from Nubia

ROYAL BRACELET
Made for Prince Nemareth, the bracelet has a central design showing the god Horus as a child (p. 27). He is sitting on a lotus and is protected by cobras. Like many children in Egyptian art, he is portrayed sucking his finger.

Hieroglyphs give name of owner

Cowrie shell shows wish of wearer to have children

LUCKY GIRDLE
This is the surviving section of a girdle. As well as cowrie shells made of electrum (a form of gold that contains a high proportion of silver), it contains beads of carnelian, amethyst, lapis lazuli, and turquoise.

A STAR IS BORN
This star was worn on the forehead as a diadem. Made of gold, it dates from the Roman period of Egypt. The Roman mummy mask shows a priest wearing a diadem.

Gold diadem

EAR ORNAMENTS
Middle Eastern influence led the Egyptians to have their ear lobes pierced and wear earrings. These earrings show how large the perforations had to be for these studs of the 14th century BCE.

Gold earrings

Faience stud

Glass stud

Jasper stud

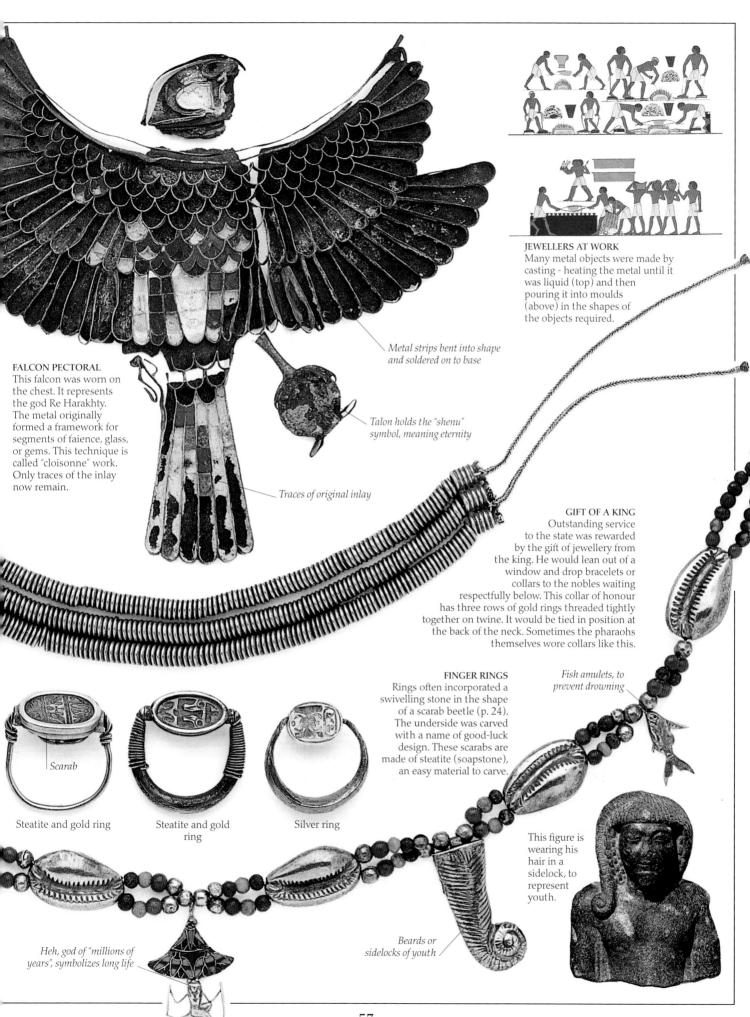

FALCON PECTORAL
This falcon was worn on the chest. It represents the god Re Harakhty. The metal originally formed a framework for segments of faience, glass, or gems. This technique is called "cloisonne" work. Only traces of the inlay now remain.

Traces of original inlay

Metal strips bent into shape and soldered on to base

Talon holds the "shenu" symbol, meaning eternity

JEWELLERS AT WORK
Many metal objects were made by casting - heating the metal until it was liquid (top) and then pouring it into moulds (above) in the shapes of the objects required.

GIFT OF A KING
Outstanding service to the state was rewarded by the gift of jewellery from the king. He would lean out of a window and drop bracelets or collars to the nobles waiting respectfully below. This collar of honour has three rows of gold rings threaded tightly together on twine. It would be tied in position at the back of the neck. Sometimes the pharaohs themselves wore collars like this.

FINGER RINGS
Rings often incorporated a swivelling stone in the shape of a scarab beetle (p. 24). The underside was carved with a name of good-luck design. These scarabs are made of steatite (soapstone), an easy material to carve.

Scarab

Steatite and gold ring

Steatite and gold ring

Silver ring

Fish amulets, to prevent drowning

This figure is wearing his hair in a sidelock, to represent youth.

Heh, god of "millions of years", symbolizes long life

Beards or sidelocks of youth

Adorning the body

THE EGYPTIANS were lovers of beauty and fashion. Many of their personal names are based on the word "nefer", meaning beautiful - for example, Nefret, Nefertiti, and Nefertari. The goddess associated with adornment was "Hathor the Golden", who is seen as the ideal of beauty in love poetry of the time. Egyptian men and women used eye paint, which was made from minerals ground on fine slate palettes. They went to great lengths in adorning themselves with cosmetics, wigs, floral garlands, and fine linen. Many objects like combs, mirrors, and cosmetic holders have survived to show how important personal appearance was to them. "Put myrrh on your head and dress up in beautiful clothes" says one Egyptian song.

Malachite

Tube with royal inscription

APPLICATORS
These were used for scooping, mixing, and applying pigment.

CRAFTSMAN'S MASTERPIECE
The mother duck's back wings slide across to give access to the face cream inside.

CONTAINERS
Ground mineral for eyepaint was mixed with water and kept in tubes like these. The one with the royal inscription may have been a gift to a courtier.

PERFUME POMADES
Courtiers tied cones of scented animal fat to their wigs, sometimes with a lotus blossom. The fat would melt and slide down the wig.

Pot made of the rare stone anhydrite

MIRROR
Courtiers used polished bronze or copper mirrors. Here a naked servant girl holding a bird forms the handle, suggesting love and beauty.

Galena

Polished metal reflective surface

Iron oxide

BATH AND MASSAGE
This noblewoman kneels on a mat while a friend holds a flower for her to smell. Her bath is symbolized by water being scattered over her; she is also being given a shoulder massage.

Tweezers

PIGMENTS
From malachite, a copper ore, the Egyptians produced green eye paint to symbolize fertility. The lead ore known as galena gave a greyblack eye paint (today often called "kohl"). Cheeks could be rouged and lips painted red by using ochres made of oxides of iron that occur plentifully throughout Egypt. Some fat would probably be mixed with the make-up when it was applied to the face.

PLUCKING AND CURLING
Priests and women used tweezers to remove hair. Women also curled their hair with tongs.

Hair curler

Double ends for different sized curls

CLOSE SHAVE
Bronze or copper razors were probably as uncomfortable to use as they look, unless in the hands of the professional travelling barbers of ancient Egypt.

FLORAL SPOON
The handle of this container represents a bunch of flowers tied together with buds of ivory stained a light pink. The top swivels to reveal or cover the cosmetic.

WOODEN COMB
Most Egyptians did not have long hair, but their wigs could be quite long and heavy, sometimes with three different layers of curls and fringes, so they needed ivory and wooden combs.

TOUCHING UP
A noblewoman called Ipwet appears in this relief. She holds a mirror while she dabs powder on to her cheeks.

HAIRPINS
These could be used to keep elaborate curls in position or hold perfume pomades in place on wigs.

Animals of the Nile Valley

PEEK-A-BOO
The goddess Hathor
was often portrayed
as a cow in the
papyrus marshes.

LION
The lion
represented
strength and
domination, and so
became an emblem of
the god-king himself.
Rarely is the lion shown
being hunted by any
other person than the
pharaoh. This gold lion
was originally part of
a necklace.

THE ANCIENT EGYPTIANS shared their environment with
many different beasts, birds, reptiles, and fish. Out in the
desert east and west of the Nile Valley you would find
ferocious lions and wild bulls as well as timid antelopes
and gazelles. These animals either hunted their prey or
grazed on the margins of the flood plain. The stillness of
night would suddenly be broken by the eerie howls of the
scavenging hyenas and jackals fighting over carcasses. In the
papyrus thickets beside the Nile there would be nests of birds
like pintail ducks, cormorants, pelicans, and hoopoes. Lurking on the river
banks would be crocodiles and in the water you might see hippos with Nile
perch and catfish darting around them. Animals appear on many ancient
Egyptian objects. They were thought of as part of the "world
system" made by the sun god, and as the earthly
versions of many gods. Animal
symbols were also used
in hieroglyphics.

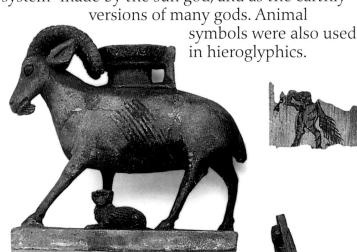

ANIMAL ANTICS
Satirical papyri show the Egyptian topsy-turvy sense of humour.
Two enemies, the antelope and the lion, are enjoying a friendly
game of senet (p. 53). A jackal playing a double flute escorts a herd
of goats while in front a cat lovingly attends to some geese. The
lion at the end seems to be amusing himself at the antics of an
ox on a couch.

WILD SHEEP AND NONCHALANT CAT
On this cosmetic container a wild sheep, or moufflon, is
stepping carefully over a crouching cat that is clearly
determined not to move. Rams symbolized some of the
most important gods in ancient Egypt. A curly-horned
ram could represent Amun-Re, King of the gods.

*Crown of Osiris,
made up of ram
horns, reeds, and
ostrich feathers.*

CROCODILE-GOD
The peril of being
snatched and eaten
by crocodiles led
the Egyptians to
try to get these
dangerous
creatures on
their side.
Consequently
the crocodile
became the
symbol of the
god Sobek, and
priests used to
decorate sacred
crocodiles with
jewellery and
mummify them
when they died.

HIPPOS
Nothing illustrates the Egpytian
fondness for visual humour quite so
much as their models of standing
hippos. The male hippo was a creature
of evil omen because of its association
with the god Seth, arch-enemy of
Osiris and Horus, rightful rulers of
Egypt. In reality, hippos could easily
overturn a papyrus boat and were
often hunted for this reason.

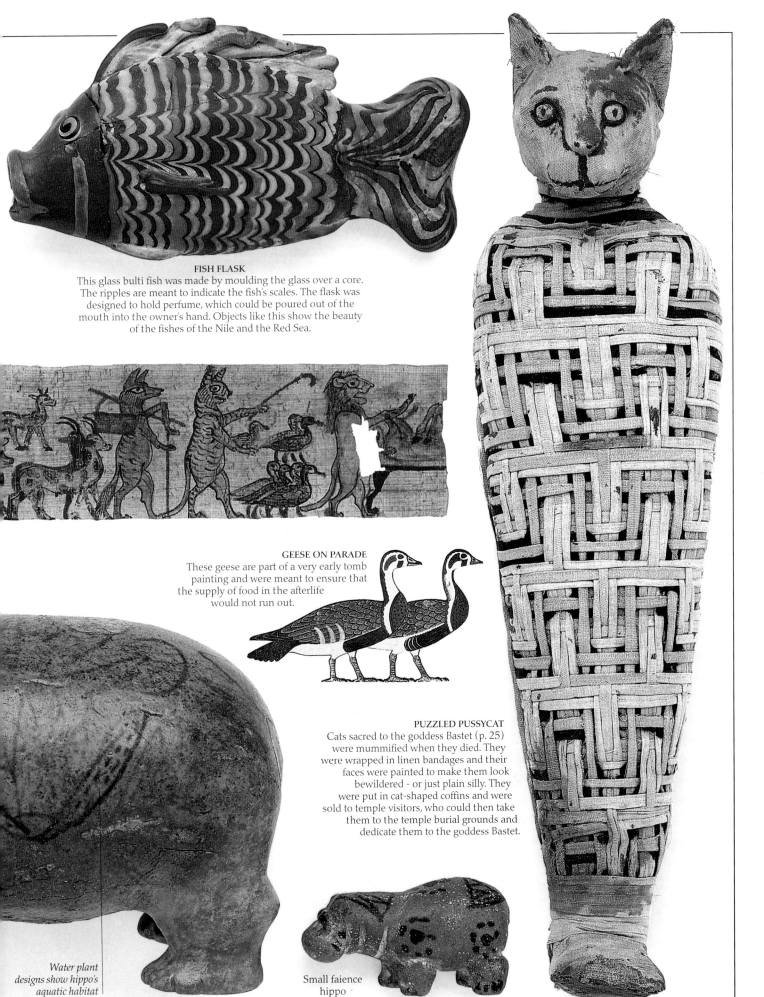

FISH FLASK
This glass bulti fish was made by moulding the glass over a core. The ripples are meant to indicate the fish's scales. The flask was designed to hold perfume, which could be poured out of the mouth into the owner's hand. Objects like this show the beauty of the fishes of the Nile and the Red Sea.

GEESE ON PARADE
These geese are part of a very early tomb painting and were meant to ensure that the supply of food in the afterlife would not run out.

PUZZLED PUSSYCAT
Cats sacred to the goddess Bastet (p. 25) were mummified when they died. They were wrapped in linen bandages and their faces were painted to make them look bewildered - or just plain silly. They were put in cat-shaped coffins and were sold to temple visitors, who could then take them to the temple burial grounds and dedicate them to the goddess Bastet.

Water plant designs show hippo's aquatic habitat

Small faience hippo

Egypt after the pharaohs

EGYPT WAS INVADED by foreigners several times in the last 1,000 years BCE. The invaders included the Sudanese, the Persians, and the Macedonians under Alexander the Great. Alexander was followed by his general Ptolemy, who founded a dynasty that ruled from Alexandria. These rulers spoke Greek and worshiped Greek gods and goddesses, but on temple walls they were portrayed as traditional Egyptian rulers. In 30 BCE Egypt passed into Roman hands and gradually, following the conversion to Christianity of the Roman emperors, churches and monasteries replaced the temples. The Arab invasion of the 7th century CE turned Egypt into the mainly Muslim country that it is today.

CLEOPATRA
Queen Cleopatra VII was the last in a line of Greek rulers of Egypt. Her suicide was famous, but there is no historical evidence to back up the familiar story that she died of the bite of a snake called an asp.

The Romans

The Roman world took grain from Egypt's fields and gold from its mines. But although the Romans exploited Egypt they also built temples. You can see the names of emperors like Augustus and Tiberius written in hieroglyphs just like those of the pharaohs, and even wearing elaborate Egyptian crowns.

EMPEROR AS HORUS
Just as the Egyptian pharaoh was identified with the god Horus (p. 27), so the Roman emperors were sometimes portrayed as this hawk-headed god. The hawk's feathers suggest metal armour and the figure wears Roman sandals and a toga.

Mummy of Artemidorus

Roman child's mummy

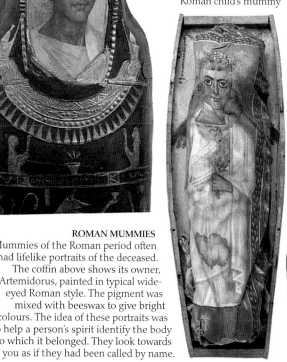

ROMAN MUMMIES
Mummies of the Roman period often had lifelike portraits of the deceased. The coffin above shows its owner, Artemidorus, painted in typical wide-eyed Roman style. The pigment was mixed with beeswax to give bright colours. The idea of these portraits was to help a person's spirit identify the body to which it belonged. They look towards you as if they had been called by name.

The Christians

Although there were Christian hermits living in caves in Egypt beforehand, Egypt officially turned to Christianity with the conversion of the Roman Empire in 324 CE. The version of Christianity that eventually triumphed in Egypt was called Coptic. It still flourishes in the country today and Coptic monks still live in thriving monasteries. Recently the relics of St Mark, who is said to have introduced Christianity into Egypt, were sent back from Venice to Cairo.

Tapestry roundel showing the victorious St George

SURVIVOR
Qasr Ibrim, a mountain in Nubia, was the centre of a Christian diocese that was stormed by Muslim troops. This silver cross was one of the items to survive the attack.

WARRIOR SAINT
The image of the god Horus on horseback spearing his rival Seth was adopted by the early Christians in Egypt to portray warrior saints like St George and St Menas.

STREET SCENE
Up to the 19th century the streets of Cairo contained stalls - each selling the products of one craft - running alongside the walls, minarets, and domes of the mosques.

Brass openwork design

The Muslims

Arab armies, skilled in warfare on horseback, conquered Egypt in the 7th century CE. They ruled through the existing, mainly Christian, bureaucracy. But Islam became the state religion, Arabic the official language, and the new city of el- Qahira later became the capital, Cairo. Eventually Egypt was conquered by the Turks and it was not until the 1960s that the country was again governed by a native Egyptian.

INCENSE BURNER
Made about 1,000 years ago this vessel was used in a mosque. Burning incense was part of the ritual of purity (which included washing and removing shoes on entering a mosque) that Muslims observed.

Did you know?

FASCINATING FACTS

Priests performing funeral rituals

Because the rituals of death and preparation for the afterlife were so elaborate in ancient Egypt, we know more about how people died than how they lived their everyday lives.

During embalming, the stomach, intestines, lungs, and liver were removed, but the heart was left in place. It was thought to contain a record of past deeds, and therefore it could determine who would be admitted to the afterlife.

Egyptians believed that the hearts and souls of those who did not pass into the afterlife would be consumed by Ammut, the Devourer of the Dead.

One of Tutankhamun's three mummiform (mummy-shaped) coffins

Pharaohs could have several wives, but only one of them would be Queen. Many pharaohs married their sisters, both to reinforce their dynastic claim to the throne and to echo the behaviour of the gods, who were believed to favour this practice.

Egyptian gods were thought to have beards, so false beards were worn by pharaohs - even female pharaohs - as a symbol of royalty.

The Great Sphinx has been buried in sand up to the neck for most of its history: it was not cleared completely until 1926. Since airborne pollution is now seriously eroding its stone body, many conservationists think it was better off covered up.

The soles of pharaohs' sandals were sometimes decorated with drawings of their enemies, who would be crushed underfoot symbolically with every step.

When King Tutankhamun's tomb was discovered in 1922, Egyptian-inspired clothing, make-up, and jewellery suddenly became the height of fashion, and even interior and graphic design reflected the contemporary fascination with ancient Egypt.

Tomb robbers were sometimes the same men who had built the tombs in the first place. They could make a fortune from selling what they stole, but if they were caught, they suffered an excruciating death impaled on a sharp wooden stake.

The need to bring organization to the first settlements along the Nile led to the invention of hieroglyphics, or picture-writing. Recent excavations suggest that these were in use several centuries before the earliest writing in Mesopotamia, which is thought to be the "cradle of civilization".

The extravagant and colourful eye make-up associated with ancient Egypt was worn by men as well as women; it was made from ground minerals mixed with water and stored in tubes.

Cleopatra was Macedonian Greek by birth. Highly educated, she spoke seven languages fluently (including Egyptian), but she usually used Greek for official documents.

False beard is a symbol of royalty

QUESTIONS AND ANSWERS

Q How did we get our information about ancient Egypt?

A Much of our knowledge comes from wall paintings, which show us how people looked, what kind of work they did, the tools they used, and how they furnished their homes. Written records tell us about daily life, religion, and government and provide facts about individual pharaohs and other important figures. Everyday objects and fabulous treasures from specific archaeological sites (particularly the tomb of Tutankhamun) also reveal details of life in the land of the Nile thousands of years ago.

Q Why did the Egyptians take so much trouble to preserve their dead as mummies?

A They believed that if a dead person's spirit could recognize his or her own preserved body, the spirit could reinhabit the body and live forever in the afterlife. For this reason, most of the internal organs were carefully removed and preserved. The brain, however, was scooped out bit by bit with a long hook pushed up one nostril; because nobody was aware of its importance, it was thrown away.

Hook to extract brain

304-09

Embalming knife

Q How was King Tutankhamun's mummy stored in his tomb?

A When it was discovered, the mummy itself was inside a huge multi-layered container. There were three coffins, one inside the other, which all fitted inside a stone sarcophagus. This sarcophagus lay inside four nesting box-like shrines, all extravagantly gilded and covered with inscriptions and intricate decoration.

Q What is the curse of King Tutankhamun?

A An ancient Egyptian curse was said to declare, "Death comes on wings to he who enters a pharaoh's tomb". Although Howard Carter and Lord Carnarvon, the men who discovered Tutankhamun's tomb, did not believe in this curse (and it eventually turned out to be a press invention), several people connected with the excavation did die within a short space of time. Among these was Lord Carnarvon himself, who nicked a mosquito bite shaving and died from a resulting infection.

Tomb painting from Thebes c.1450 BCE

Q Why did the ancient Egyptians associate the colour black with life rather than death?

A Because the Nile earth that sustained them was so rich it was almost black, the Egyptians saw black as the colour of life; while red, which resembled the barren desert, represented bad fortune. Green, the colour of crops before they ripen, symbolized resurrection in the afterlife.

Q How did Egyptian rulers pay for their extravagant pyramids, temples and palaces?

A Ancient Egypt was very wealthy. Although only about ten percent of the land was suitable for farming, it produced far more food than the people needed, so they could sell the excess abroad. Mostly, though, the earth's riches were in the form of semi-precious stones and mineral deposits – especially gold.

Q What role did women play in ancient Egyptian society?

A Although females tended to take on their husband's status in society, they were equal with men in law and therefore allowed to own or rent property, engage in business, inherit money, get divorced and remarried, and even reign as pharaoh. The last pharaoh to rule Egypt before the country came under the control of Imperial Rome was a woman – the legendary Cleopatra.

Life-sized statue of King Djoser

Gold amulet case

Record Breakers

RECORD REIGN
The longest reign of any ruler in history is that of the pharaoh Pepy II. He came to the throne when he was six years old in 2278 BCE and he was still ruling when he died in 2184 BCE at age 100 – 94 years later.

CHANGELESS SOCIETY
The civilization of ancient Egypt lasted for more than 3,000 years, during which time its culture and way of life remained largely unchanged.

FIRST AMONG NATIONS
Founded in 3100 BCE by King Narmer (sometimes identified with King Menes), Egypt was the world's first nation state.

ANCIENT IMAGE
The earliest almost life-sized portrait in existence is a seated statue of King Djoser (2667–2648 BCE), which was found in an enclosed chamber attached to the side of his pyramid.

The pharaohs

THE ANCIENT EGYPTIANS dated events to a particular year in the reign of a king or pharaoh (this is called regnal dating). A scholar named Manetho, who lived during the Ptolemaic era, later sorted the kings into dynasties, a system that is still used today. The resulting chronology is not exact or complete, however, and it is subject to change when new discoveries are made.

Queen Nefertiti

EARLY DYNASTIC PERIOD

c.3100–2890 BCE		c.2890–2686 BCE	
1ST DYNASTY		**2ND DYNASTY**	
Narmer	3100	Hetepsekhemwy	2890
Aha	3100	Raneb	2865
Djer	3000	Nynetjer	
Djet	2980	Weneg	
Den	2950	Sened	
Anedjib	2925	Peribsen	2700
Semerkhet	2900	Khasekhemwy	2686
Qaa	2890		

aka Amenhotep IV   † aka Amenophis
* denotes female pharaoh   ‡ aka Sesostris
** aka Thutmose

FIRST INTERMEDIATE PERIOD

c.2181–2125 BCE	c.2160–2055 BCE
7TH & 8TH DYNASTIES During this unstable period of Egyptian history there were many temporary kings. Also, the weakening of central power meant that local dynasties became established.	**9TH & 10TH DYNASTIES HERAKLEOPOLITAN** Kheti Merykare Ity **11TH DYNASTY (THEBES ONLY)** Intef I 2125–2112 Intef II 2112–2063 Intef III 2063–2055

MIDDLE KINGDOM

c.2055–1985 BCE	
11TH DYNASTY ALL EGYPT	
Montuhotep II	055–2004
Montuhotep III	2004–1992
Montuhotep IV	1992–1985

Montuhotep II

NEW KINGDOM

c.1550–1295 BCE		c.1295–1186 BCE		c.1186–1069 BCE	
18TH DYNASTY		**19TH DYNASTY**		**20TH DYNASTY**	
Ahmose	1550–1525	Ramesses I	1295–1294	Sethnakhte	1186–1184
Amenhotep I †	1525–1504	Seti I	1294–1279	Ramesses III	1184–1153
Tuthmosis I**	1504–1492	Ramses II	1279–1213	Ramesses IV	1153–1147
Tuthmosis II**	1492–1479	Merneptah	1213–1203	Ramesses V	1147–1143
Tuthmosis III**	1479–1425	Amenmessul	203–1200	Ramesses VI	1143–1136
Hatshepsut*	1473–1458	Seti II	1200–1194	Ramesses VII	1136–1129
Amenhotep II †	1427–1400	Saptah	1194–1188	Ramesses VIII	1129–1126
Tuthmosis IV**	1400–1390	Tawosret*	1188–1186	Ramesses IX	1126–1108
Amenhotep III †	1390–1352			Ramesses X	1108–1099
Akhenaten #	1352–1336			Ramesses XI	1099–1069
Nefertiti					
Smenkhkare*	1338–1336				
Tutankhamun	1336–1327				
Ay	1327–1323				
Horemheb	1323–1295				

Ramesses the Great

LATE PERIOD

c.672–525 BCE		c.525–359 BCE		c.404–380 BCE		c.380–343 BCE	
26TH DYNASTY		**27TH DYNASTY (PERSIAN PERIOD 1)**		**28TH DYNASTY**		**30TH DYNASTY**	
Nekau I	672–664			Amyrtaios	404–399	Nectanebo I	380–362
Psamtek I	664–610	Cambyses	525–522			Teos	362–360
Nekau II	610–595	Darius I	522–486	**29TH DYNASTY**		Nectanebo II	360–343
Psamtek II	595–589	Xerxes I	486–465	Nepherites I	399–393		
Apries	589–570	Artaxerxes I	465–424	Hakor	393–380		
Ahmose II	570–526	Darius II	424–405	Nepherites II	c.380		
Psamtek III	526–525	Artaxerxes II	405–359				

OLD KINGDOM

c.2686–2613 BCE

3RD DYNASTY

Sanakht	2686–2667
Djoser	2667–2648
Sekhemkhet	2648–2640
Khaba	2640–2637
Huni	2637–2613

Giza Pyramids

c.2613–2494 BCE

4TH DYNASTY

Sneferu	2613–2589
Khufu	2589–2566
Radjedef	2566–2558
Khafra	2558–2532
Menkaura	2532–2503
Shepseskaf	2503–2494

c.2494–2345 BCE

5TH DYNASTY

Userkaf	2494–2487
Sahura	2487–2475
Neferirkara	2475–2455
Shepseskara	2455–2448
Raneferef	2448–2445
Nyuserra	2445–2421
Menkauhor	2421–2414
Djedkara	2414–2375
Unas	2375–2345

c.2345–2181 BCE

6TH DYNASTY

Teti	2345–2323
Userkara	2323–2321
Pepy I	2321–2287
Merenre	2287–2278
Pepy II	2278–2184
Nitocris*	2184–2181

SECOND INTERMEDIATE PERIOD

c.1985–1795 BCE

12TH DYNASTY

Amenemhat I	1985–1955
Senusret I ‡	1965–1920
Amenemhat II	1922–1878
Senusret II ‡	1880–1874
Senusret III ‡	1874–1855
Amenemhat III	1855–1808
Amenemhat IV	1808–1799
Sobekneferu*	1799–1795

Overlaps in dates indicate periods of co-regency

c.1795–1650 BCE

13TH DYNASTY

1795–c.1725

14TH DYNASTY

1750–1650

Minor figures who ruled at the same time as the 13th dynasty

c.1650–1550 BCE

15TH DYNASTY

Salitis	
Khyan	1600
Apepi	1555
Khamudi	

16TH DYNASTY

1650–1550

Minor Hyksos kings who ruled at the same time as the 15th Dynasty

c.1650–1550 BCE

17TH DYNASTY

In addition to the pharaohs of the 15th and 16th dynasties, several kings ruled from Thebes including the following:

Intef	
Ta I	
Seqenenre Taa II	c.1560
Kamose	1555–1550

THIRD INTERMEDIATE PERIOD

c.1069–945 BCE

21ST DYNASTY

Smendes	1069–1043
Amenemnisu	1043–1039
Psusennes I	1039–991
Amenemope	993–984
Osorkon the Elder	984–978
Siamun	978–959
Psusennes II	959–945

c.945–715 BCE

22ND DYNASTY

Sheshonq I	945–924
Osorkon I	924–889
Sheshonq II	c.890
Takelot I	889–874
Osorkon II	874–850
Takelot II	850–825
Sheshonq III	825–773
Pimay	773–767
Sheshonq V	767–730
Osorkon IV	730–715

c.818–715 BCE

23RD DYNASTY

Several continuous lines of rulers based at Herakleopolis Magna, Hermopolis Magna, Leontopolis and Tanis, including the following:

Pedubastist I	818–793
Sheshonq IV	c.780
Osorkon III	777–749

24TH DYNASTY

Bakenrenef	727–715

LATE PERIOD

c.747–656 BCE

25TH DYNASTY

Piy	747–716
Shabaqo	716–702
Shabitqo	702–690
Taharqo	690–664
Tanutamani	664–656

Ivory sphinx

PTOLEMAIC PERIOD

c.343–332 BCE

PERSIAN PERIOD 2

Artaxerxes III Ochus	343–338
Arses	338–336
Darius III Codoman	336–332

c.332–305 BCE

MACEDONIAN DYNASTY

Alexander the Great	332–323
Philip Arrhidaeus	323–317
Alexander IV	317–305

Lotus flower motif

c.305–80 BCE

PTOLEMAIC DYNASTY

Ptolemy I	305–285
Ptolemy II	285–246
Ptolemy III	246–221
Ptolemy IV	221–205
Ptolemy V	205–180
Ptolemy VI	180–145
Ptolemy VII	145
Ptolemy VIII	170–116
Ptolemy IX	116–107
Ptolemy X	107–88
Ptolemy IX	88–80

c.80–30 BCE

PTOLEMAIC DYNASTY (CONT.)

Ptolemy XI	80
Ptolemy XII	80–51
Cleopatra VII*	51–30
Ptolemy XIII	51–47
Ptolemy XIV	47–44
Ptolemy XV	44–30

Egypt became part of the Roman Empire in 30 BCE

Map labels

MEDITERRANEAN SEA

NILE DELTA

LOWER EGYPT

Abu Rawash
Zawyet el-Aryan
Great Sphinx
N. and S. Saqqara
Giza
Abusir
Mazghuna
el-Lisht
Saila
Meidum
Hawara
Kahun (Lahum)

RED SEA

Zawyet el-Maiyitin

UPPER EGYPT

River Nile

Dara

Tukh (Nubt)

Ancient
Egypt

el-Kula
Edfu

Find out more

IF YOU'RE INSPIRED to explore the mysteries of ancient Egypt even further, check out your local museum to see if it has a specialist collection worth visiting. You can also use the internet to investigate the many websites devoted to the land of the pharaohs.

One of the world's finest Egyptian collections is housed in the Egyptian Museum in Cairo. Founded by a Frenchman, Auguste Mariette, in 1863, this institution owns over 250,000 objects, less than half of which are on show at any one time. The most famous items are undoubtedly artefacts unearthed from the tomb of King Tutankhamun, but the museum also has exhibits that illuminate every period of the country's ancient history from 3100 BCE to the second century CE.

Vulture and cobra symbols

EGYPTIAN MUSEUM
Situated in the centre of Cairo, the Egyptian Museum does not look particularly large, but its thousands of exhibits are very densely packed. The present building, opened in 1902, was designed specifically for this collection, which had outgrown two sites since it was established in 1863.

THE SPHINX
The earliest known monumental sculpture in Egypt, the Sphinx once had a false beard. Like the nose, however, it was lost many centuries ago. Some experts believe the beard was not added until hundreds of years after the statue was built, around 2500 BCE.

FINE JEWELLERY

Made out of gold and semi-precious stones from the rich Nile earth, ancient Egyptian jewellery displays a sophisticated design sense and an advanced level of craftsmanship. The Egyptian Museum in Cairo, the Metropolitan Museum in New York, and the British Museum in London all have impressive pieces on display.

Gold rings

Anubis, jackal god of embalming

Section of a girdle

Fish-shaped amulet

Gold star from diadem (headband)

KING'S COFFIN

Tutankhamun's mummy was placed in three nesting coffins, all glimmering with gold. The middle or second coffin, which is on display in the Egyptian Museum, is made of gilded wood inlaid with crimson and turquoise glass and blue pottery.

EGYPT AMERICAN STYLE

Constructed in an Egyptian style, the Luxor hotel in Las Vegas contains an artificial river Nile, virtual reality settings and plastic palm trees (above). The hotel is built in a dramatic pyramid shape 30 storeys tall, and is guarded by a replica of the Giza Sphinx that is actually bigger than the real one.

USEFUL WEBSITES

- Specialist site run by the British Museum
  www.ancientegypt.co.uk
- British Museum site for children, to explore collections held at the museum with printable activities
  www.thebritishmuseunt.ac.uk/childrenscompass
- An exploration of Egyptian art and timeline, run by the Metropolitan Museum
  www.metmuseum.org/explore/newegypt/htm/a-index.htm
- Award-winning site from the Museum of Fine Art, Boston
  www.mfa.org/egypt
- Ancient Egypt section of the Royal Ontario Museum site
  www.rom.on.ca/programs/activities/egypt/learn/

Crook and flail

HOUSEHOLD OBJECTS

Made from coloured ceramic in about 1450 BCE, this wide-bodied jar adorned with ducks is typical of the ancient Egyptian artefacts on view in many museums.

Places to visit

EGYPTIAN MUSEUM, CAIRO, EGYPT

Although this is not an enormous museum, it has a spectacular display of antiquities including:
- the Tutankhamun collection, set in its own galleries, which contain around 1,700 items relating to the boy king, such as his fabulous gold funeral mask
- the Royal Mummy Room, where the remains of great rulers such as Ramses II, Seti I, and Thuthmosis II can be seen
(Also worth visiting are the Luxor Museum and the Mummification Museum, which are both in Luxor.)

BRITISH MUSEUM, LONDON, UK

This museum has the largest and most comprehensive collection of ancient Egyptian art and artefacts outside Cairo, which includes:
- the Rosetta stone, the key to deciphering ancient Egyptian hieroglyphics
- a gallery of monumental sculpture containing a statue of Rameses II
- an impressive display of mummies and coffins

METROPOLITAN MUSEUM OF ART, NEW YORK, USA

The impressive Egyptian collection owned by "The Met" takes up a considerable area of the museum's vast ground floor, and includes:
- sculptures of the infamous Queen Hatshepsut, who seized power in the sixteenth century BCE
- more than 20 tiny, perfect models from the tomb of a nobleman called Mekutra
- a large collection of jewellery

MUSEUM OF FINE ARTS, BOSTON, USA

Consisting of more than 40,000 items, this display attracts visitors and scholars from around the world. Among its attractions are:
- a superb collection of ancient artefacts, which archaeologists collected from their original setting
- a charmingly lifelike double statue of King Menkaura and his favourite wife, Khamerernebty

ROYAL ONTARIO MUSEUM, TORONTO, CANADA

The Egyptian gallery in this museum traces Egypt's history from 4000 BCE to 324 CE and features:
- computer animation that takes visitors inside the Great Pyramid
- the mummy of a temple musician who died in about 850 BCE from an abscessed tooth

Glossary

ADZE Ancient Egyptian tool for carving and planing wood.

AMULET Charm used to ward off evil.

ANCIENT EGYPT The period when Egypt was ruled by pharaohs, which was between around 3100 BCE and 30 BCE.

ANKH Ancient Egyptian symbol of life, which, traditionally, only gods and royalty carried.

ANTECHAMBER Small room that leads to a bigger or more important one.

ARCHAEOLOGY The study of human history through the excavation and analysis of objects and artefacts.

BA The essence of a deceased person's personality, often represented by his or her head on the body of a hawk, (*see also* KA)

BRECCIA Mottled rock formed of separate stones cemented together in lime, and used for carving pots and vases.

CANOPIC JAR Special container for storing one of the internal organs from a dead body.

Canopic jars

CARTOUCHE In Egyptology, an oval border around a Pharaoh's names.

CASSIA Bark from a type of laurel tree, dried and used in perfume and incense.

CATARACT Powerful rush of water around a large rock that blocks a river's flow. There are several cataracts along the Nile, and important monuments were often sited near them.

CROOK Royal symbol in the form of a hooked shepherd's staff representing kingship. (*see also* FLAIL)

Ankh

DELTA The roughly triangular-shaped area of deposited earth at the mouth of a river. Since the Nile runs through a vast desert, Egyptians have always relied heavily on the rich soil of its delta and river valley for farming.

DEMOTIC SCRIPT A popular and rapid form of writing based on hieratic script, (*see also* HIERATIC SCRIPT and HIEROGLYPHS)

DYNASTY Succession of rulers from related families.

EMBALMING The preservation of a dead body from decay using chemicals, salts, perfumes, and ointments.

FINIAL Decorative emblem or knob on the end of a pole.

FLAIL Royal symbol in the form of a corn-threshing implement representing the fertility of the land. (*see also* CROOK)

FLAX Flowering plant cultivated for its textile fibres, which are spun into linen cloth.

Crook

Flail

Statue from Karnak with crook and flail

FRANKINCENSE Fragrant gum resin burned as incense. It comes from trees of the genus *Boswellia*.

Henna

GIRDLE Belt or cord worn low on the waist and often adorned with precious stones, shells, silver and gold.

HENNA Dried and ground-up leaves of a tropical shrub used to colour hair and skin and believed by the ancient Egyptians to protect against danger.

HIERATIC SCRIPT A simplified version of hieroglyphs, (*see also* HIEROGLYPHS and DEMOTIC SCRIPT)

HIEROGLYPHS Picture writing used to build up words in ancient Egyptian script. (*see also* HIERATIC SCRIPT and DEMOTIC SCRIPT)

INCENSE Gum or spice that is burned to create sweet-smelling smoke. The Egyptians used incense in their religious rituals and to purify the air in the temple.

KA A dead person's spirit, which the ancient Egyptians believed could bring his or her body back to life. (*see also* BA)

KHAT Bag-like cover worn over a pharaoh's wig.

Lotus flower

KOHL Black powder used to create dramatic eye make-up by men, women and children in ancient Egypt.

LAPIS LAZULI Bright blue semi-precious stone widely used in Egyptian jewellery and artefacts.

LOTUS Waterlily whose shape - often highly stylized - was widely employed as a decorative device in ancient Egypt.

MUMMY Dead body that has been preserved from decay, either naturally or by artificial means.

NATRON Moisture-absorbing salt used to dry a corpse before it was wrapped in bandages.

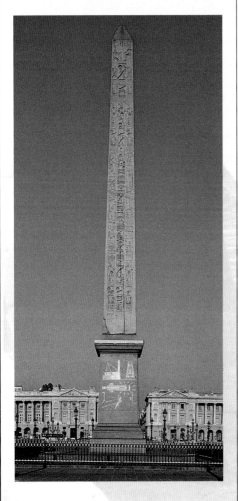

Egyptian obelisk in Paris

NEMES Special striped headcloth worn by Egyptian kings. In his famous death mask, King Tutankhamun is wearing a dramatic gold and blue nemes.

NOME One of 42 administrative districts of ancient Egypt, each of which had its own god.

OBELISK Tapered stone column with a square or rectangular base and sloping sides rising to a pointed tip.

PALETTE Flat surface on which colours were mixed to make either writing pigments or cosmetics.

PAPYRUS Tall riverside reed whose stem was widely used to make baskets, sandals, boats, rope, and paper-like sheets or scrolls. Papyrus was the main material for writing on in ancient Egypt.

PECTORAL Ornamental pendant or similar piece of jewellery, often decorated with a metal strip framework inset with coloured glass or semi-precious stones.

PHARAOH The title given to the rulers of ancient Egypt. The word pharaoh means "great house", and originally referred to the palace rather than the king.

PYRAMID Massive stone structure with a square base and sloping sides. In Egypt, pyramids were usually royal tombs, but some may have other purposes.

REGENT Court official or minor royal - often the king's mother - appointed to rule on behalf of a very young or incapacitated pharaoh.

SARCOPHAGUS Elaborate and massive outer stone coffin.

SCARAB Sacred dung beetle that symbolized the sun-god Khepri.

SCRIBE Government official who, unlike most ordinary people, could both read and write.

SENET Egyptian board game based on the struggle between good and evil.

SHABTI Figures made in the image of servants, and buried with important people so they could perform any manual tasks required in the afterlife.

SHADUF Pole with bucket and counterweight used for raising water from the Nile to fill irrigation canals.

SHRINE Container for holding the statue of a god or the remains of a dead body; a place dedicated to the memory of a dead person.

SICKLE Crescent-shaped tool with a cutting edge (usually made of flint) on the inside, used for harvesting grain.

SIDELOCK Section of tressed hair anchored on one side of the head in order to indicate the youth of the wearer.

SISTRUM Ceremonial rattle carried by noble women and priestesses.

SITULA Sacred vessel that contained holy water for the temple.

SNAKE Egyptian game involving counters and a circular stone board that represented a snake coiled around its own head.

SOUL HOUSE Miniature model dwelling placed in the tomb of its dead owner for use in the afterlife.

SPHINX In ancient Egypt, the sphinx was a monumental creature with a lion's body and the head of the ruler. Sphinxes were believed to guard the entrances to the underworld on both the eastern and the western horizons.

Shabti figures

STELA Upright stone slab or pillar covered with carving or inscriptions.

THROWSTICK Wooden hunting instrument similar to a boomerang, used to stun, injure or kill prey.

TOMB Grave, monument, or building where the body of a dead person is laid.

UNDERWORLD Abode of the dead, thought to lie deep under the earth.

URAEUS The royal cobra, displayed by pharaohs on the front of the head. The serpent was believed to spit fire at the king's enemies.

VIZIERS Highest officials appointed by the pharaoh to rule Upper and Lower Egypt.

WEDJAT EYE Protective symbol representing the eye of Horus.

WINNOWING The process of separating chaff from grain by tossing both in the air.

Wedjat Eye

Index

Acknowledgements

Dorling Kindersley would like to thank: The Departments of Egyptian Antiquities, Oriental Antiquities, & Medieval & Later Antiquities, British Museum, for providing artefacts for photography; James Putnam for helping to arrange for artefacts to be photographed & for assisting with picture research; Celia Clear of British Museum Publications; Morgan Reid for his advice on photographic lighting; Meryl Silbert for production; Karl Shone for special photography (pp. 20-21); Lester Cheeseman for his desktop publishing expertise; Kathy Lockley for picture research.

For this edition, the publisher would also like to thank: James Putnam for assisting with updates; Claire Bowers, David Ekholm-JAlbum,

Sunita Gahir, Joanne Little, Nigel Ritchie, Susan St Louis, Carey Scott, & Bulent Yusuf for the clipart; David Ball, Neville Graham, Rose Horridge, Joanne Little, & Sue Nicholson for the wallchart; BCP, Laragh Kedwell, Marianne Petrou, & Owen Peyton Jones for checking the digitized files.

The publisher would like to thank the following for their kind permission to reproduce their images:

Picture credits a=above, b=bottom, c=centre, far=far, l=left, m=middle, r= right, t=top

Agyptisches Museum/Photo: Staatliche Museen zu Berlin: 48bl. **Ancient Art & Architecture Collection:** 10bl, 10 bm, 11tr, 11

bl, 14tr, 28–9t. **Anglo Aquarium Plant Co./ Barbara Thomas:** 26ml. **Bridgeman Art Library:** 24tr, 28tl, 28br. **British Museum:** 6b, 9tr, 10m, l lm , 14br, 15tl, 15tm, 15br, 16tr, 18m, 19t, 19br, 22tl, 26mr, 27tl, 27m, 28m, 29r, 30mr, 32, 33, 34m, 35mr, 40tl, 41t, 41bm, 44m, 45tl, 461,46b, 49bl, 50m, 51tm, 53tm, 56tl, 56bl, 57br, 58bm, 59bm, 60tr, 601m, 62bl, 62bm, 63tr. **British Museum/ Nina M. de Garis Davies:** 39m, 48mr, 51b, 61m. **Peter Clayton:** 26tl, 38m. **Bruce Coleman Ltd:** 41mr. **Michael Dixon, Photo Resources:** 10tr, 25tl. **Egypt Exploration Society, London:** 54br. **Mary Evans Picture Library:** 57tr, 62tr. **Werner Forman Archive:** 8tr. **Editions Gallimard:** 20tl. **Griffith Institute, Ashmolean Museum, Oxford:** 23b. **Robert Harding Picture Library:** 12ml, 13bl, 23mr, 24bl, 36–7b, 39tr, 42tl, 53ml, 54tl. **George Hart:** 23m, 29m. **Michael Holford:** 41br.

Hutchison Library: 9mr. Courtesy of the Oriental Institute of the University of Chicago: 44–5b. **Popperfoto:** 38tl. James Putnam: 31ml. **Louvre/© Réunion des Musées Nationaux:** 55tm. **Uni-Dia Verlag:** 43 ml. **University College, London:** 22b, 35ml. **Roger Wood:** 32tl. **Verlag Philipp von Zabern/ Cairo Museum:** 8–9b.

Illustrators: Thomas Keenes: 21tl, 32br, 33bl, 43t, 55bc; Eugene Fleury: 8cl.

Wallchart: DK Images: British Museum bc, cr (The Rosetta Stone), fcra (Papyrus), tl; Egyptian Museum, Cairo c, cra (Nefertiti); Wellcome Institute / Science Museum, London cb.

All other images © Dorling Kindersley. For further information see: www.dkimages.com